The Nearly Girl

Sophie Wright

The Nearly Girl
By Sophie Wright

Introduction

"You should write a book."

How many times have I heard that one? A lot. And how many times have I said to myself, "One day I will write a book"? Even more.

The older you get the more terrifying it is when you realise you are still putting off those things you always said you would do. One day. When you have time. When you're in the right headspace. Sometimes you just have to dive in! As blind and clueless as you may feel going into something, nothing will feel worse than thinking, "Why did I never do that?"

So here we are. I'm writing a book. Some people think I'm crazy. Others also think I'm crazy and therefore can't wait to read it. I owe it to them as well as myself. I owe it to everyone who may have gone through similar things to me. Or not as the case may be. (Things do get pretty weird at times!) but I believe there is a book in all of us.

Little did I know at the time, I actually started writing this book in my teens. I began writing a diary style journal every night, on and off for years, and well into my twenties. It was my therapy. I'd write all the things I couldn't say out loud. I'd process things, answering my own questions or heart cries as I reached the end of each page. Plus, I didn't swear in real life, but I could swear on paper. (Let that be a little disclaimer!)

While on the subject of disclaimers, everything in this book is based on real-life experiences, real-life people and real-life feelings. However, all names and venue names have

1

been changed because I don't want to get sued. Now we're clear on that, we can begin...

Chapter 1 – The Early Years

My childhood was the most beautiful, precious bubble you could imagine. If I could've just stayed there, life would've been much simpler. Supportive, loving, stable family. Parents who were still so in love, a slightly older brother I was never particularly close with – although I still had his back. Even if he did try to strangle me when I was two years old and it took both my mum and godmother to prize his little hands off my throat. It didn't help that they were both weak with laughter at the time. Clearly, I lived, but I still don't cope well with close- fitting necklines or choker necklaces to this day.

I've always been incredibly close to my mum. We were more like sisters than parent and child. She took me out of school TWICE and home-schooled me herself, when she could see the academic school system was failing me miserably, and bitchy bullies were crushing my spirit. (We'll get to that later.)

Mum was a badass. A former 'Youngest Headteacher in the borough,' reiki master, Catholic schoolgirl, hilarious storyteller, self-believer, fiercely protective of her brood and my biggest supporter and fan. Half of the crazy situations I got myself into were down to mum's encouragement. Although sometimes it turned out to be a very BAD idea... It made me love her even more.

School had always been a struggle. I couldn't keep up academically and there seemed to be no place for my creativity. Daily low scores, teachers snapping at me to "try harder," when I just didn't get it! I was feeling worse about myself on the daily, and even at 8/9 years of age, I began to feel like I wasn't good enough.

After what felt like years of pestering, I persuaded mum to take me to the local ice rink.

"But why do you want to go there?! It's cold and dirty and all the older kids congregate at the disco nights..." (Unbeknown to me, they were doing drugs.) Plus, its freezing!" She was right about all the above, of course. But we'd already tried horse riding lessons, tap dancing and playing the trumpet.*

*[Random, I know. I felt sorry for the old grey-haired man who came into class to tell us about trumpet lessons, and ask who would like to learn. When no one put their hand up, I died a little inside for him. So that night I came home with a silver trumpet and a bill for six lessons upfront. No, it didn't last long, but I did learn to play 'Good King Wenceslas' badly.]

One busy Saturday, aged 9, I took my first steps on the ice and fell in love. It felt so natural to me. I felt so free. Very quickly I was spending most weekends there and I soon caught the eye of one of the coaches. He saw potential and suggested we invest in some private lessons for me. It really wasn't in my mum's budget, but she booked me none the less. She could see how happy it was making me and this newfound feeling that I was actually good at something. Sadly, this was when I lost my skating buddy, Jessie. Her mum went all jealous and weird due to the fact I'd been 'spotted' and her daughter was still struggling with a 3-turn. (The basics!)
We stopped playing and skating together. Little did I know, her mum gave my mum a bitchy earful and started blanking her. It later transpired that Jessie did the same. We would soon learn that this behaviour among the 'Skater Mums' was referred to as 'The Mother Mafia': The pushy mums. The gossipers. The ones secretly wanting the other kids to fall as they watched with hawk eyes, lining up against the radiators,

while clutching polystyrene cups of lukewarm tea each session.

Living for my next skating session became the thing that would get me through each school day. I never had many friends at school. I was painfully shy and quiet. A dreamer, who's confidence was continually knocked by lack of academic achievements. My older brother, on the other hand, was completely different in every way. Not physical or athletic at all, but he was an absolute whizz at any type of maths or science, biology, in particular. Even to this day he would still throw back at me, "Well, I did A-Level Biology," randomly during disagreements about something totally unrelated. Sam was the year above me; but when the time came for him to go to high school, I had the opportunity to move with him.

It was no secret that I was failing miserably at school. Or what I should say is, school was failing me. I was desperately unhappy and seemingly punished for no reason by the teacher. I remember one day she decided to move the disruptive people around the class to split them up. I was quite happy where I was, in the corner by the window, where I would gaze constantly across the playing field, wishing I was somewhere else. Unfairly, she decided to move me to the centre table, next to the most hyperactive boy in the class, who would constantly kick the table as I was trying to write. He would later in life go on to arrange his own attempted murder, by joining a chat room and pretending to be multiple FBI agents. He convinced an impressionable boy his own age that he'd been 'recruited' to carry out this awful task. Thankfully, he survived his own stabbing, and a documentary was later made about the whole intricate mission he'd orchestrated... You get the picture: I'd much rather be sat next to the window and the moody kid that wouldn't make eye contact.

To this day I'm still not sure how my parents came across the somewhat unconventional school we moved onto, my brother and I. I probably should ask them. This was not your average school! A small, Christian private school with a total of 52 pupils, ranging from reception through to GCSE students. There were as little as two students in some entire year groups and parents were encouraged to volunteer in some way, albeit teaching classes, playground duties or even cleaning, in order to have their school fees waived for their child. My mum – being the amazing 'can-do' lady that she is and more qualified than all those teachers put together – taught several days a week to afford to keep me and my brother there. As weird as it was as a school, it was the best place for me at the time. I would have been eaten alive had I moved to a big comprehensive high school. Even today high school kids still terrify me... Congregating in huge groups on street corners at home time, shouting, swearing and smoking. Competing to look more 'hard' than the next kid or the rival school. I was protected from all that, able to grow and develop at my own natural pace, personality-wise and academically. Or so we'd hoped.

Chapter 2 - That's evil

I was eleven when I first went there. Let's call it King's School. Today, it's a car dealership neighbouring a large church and community centre, but at the time it was a fresh start. A clean slate where no one knew how bad I was at maths. But it didn't take long for me to realise this place was far from normal...

On my first day, one of the girls asked who my favourite band was.

"B*Witched!" I replied, enthusiastically.

"That's evil!" she snapped. "You can't listen to that."

I'm sorry what? What was she on?

"Yeah, you can't listen to that, it's of the devil," another girl said.

I was struggling to see how a four-piece girl band in matching denim, Irish dancing around a field in their music video was classed as 'devil music'. I was later asked what book I was reading.

"Harry Potter," I said.

"That's of the devil! You are not allowed to read that!" My classmate shrieked. I looked to the other girls for some clarity, but they all looked equally horrified.

Over the coming weeks, I felt the vibe towards me changing.

"New episodes of Sabrina the Teenage Witch on Nickelodeon tonight! I'm so excited!" I said, trying to make conversation and find common ground with my peers. I also really wanted to marry the guy who played Harvey.

"THE DEVIL!" – "WITCHCRAFT!" – "THAT'S EVIL!" were the replies I was met with. Great. I'm clearly not endearing myself to anyone here. When I made it known that I was from a long line of Irish Catholics, said my Hail Mary's and went to a Catholic primary school, a girl in my class went straight home to tell her mum, who promptly made a formal complaint about my mum. Complaining that we 'worshiped statues' and she shouldn't be allowed to teach here.

Looking back, I was a bit like a controversial grenade getting thrown into a group of very black-and-white, belief-steeped youngsters. Maybe I got off to a bad start? But, unbeknownst to me, I was about to get even more controversial...

The headmaster's son made it known that he had a crush on me and slipped a hand-scribbled "I heart U" note into my lunch box. I didn't really know who he was at first, but I soon got to know, as before long we were frequently passing notes to one another at any opportunity. I developed a massive crush on him in return. Looking back, this stemmed more from the fact that someone actually liked me, not who that person necessarily was. But, like any 12-year-old would do, I convinced myself I was in love with him and we would marry and have two children one day.

As word got round (which didn't take long in a school so small), it was strongly frowned upon, as you can imagine. Maybe this made the girls dislike me even more? I'd never discussed anything boy-related with them, but in their eyes, it was probably yet another thing I was doing wrong. I was mortified one day, when the headmaster picked up and read aloud one of the notes his son had not so subtly tried to throw at me in class. Always a risky idea. Especially when it's your dad teaching the class. All the other girls revelled in my embarrassment, and I was pretty much excluded from all their conversations the rest of that day. Despite all this, my little school crush was responsible for getting me through most of the boring school days, putting a real spring in my step! It became a much bigger deal in my head. Imagine how heartbroken I was when he suddenly decided he fancied one of the other girls instead and never bothered with me again. She was the complete opposite to me, and I had to watch as they would playfully slap one another, flirtingly teasing and passing similar notes during lessons and lunch breaks. Buying her chocolates for Valentine's Day and suchlike. It all seems so small looking back; but at the time, for my young head and heart to comprehend, it was huge. My first feeling of rejection. I listened to my Gabrielle cassette 'Out of Reach' a lot during that time... almost burning it out. That was my heartbreak song. We all have those tunes that snatch your breath when they catch you off guard on a random shuffle, or skipping through radio stations, causing memories to rush back and a sting of tears to flood your eyes. But when the day comes that you can listen to them and not flinch or swallow that lump in your throat, that's the day when you have fully healed. Believe me when I say that day will come. Until then, change your playlist.

Chapter 3 – Broccoli, Broccoli, Cauliflower

You would hope by now there would be some positives coming through in my school years, but I'm having to clutch at some serious straws to recall them. The main things that spring to mind were my after-school skating sessions which gave me so much life. Regardless of how my day had gone, stepping on that ice at the end of it literally melted away all my troubles. My mum teaching at my school a couple of days a week meant I could grab a hug in the corridor when I was feeling weak or alone. There were also some days where we'd all nearly miss our entire first subject, through reasons way out of our control...

Each morning the entire school would gather in the hall for worship. It was basically assembly merged with a full-on church service. Lots of Bible readings, prayers and singing and so forth It was only meant to last about 30 minutes but if the Holy Spirit moved, we would take longer and end up missing our first lesson. We were strongly encouraged to speak in tongues – something I've never understood and never to this day been able to do, but everyone else seemed to be fluent in it.

One particular morning, we were asked to put our hands up if we could not speak in tongues. I ought to have lied and sat on my hands, but as I did with the guy selling trumpet lessons, I raised my hand feeling proud of my honesty. Myself, along with only three other people, were pulled to the front, while the rest of the pupils and teachers crowded round us and laid hands on us. They started praying for us in tongues and (I'm assuming) asking that we too would be given this magical, holy gift. I felt like a tiny dot in a sea of my peers and their sweaty hands resting on my shoulders or held out above me. Their chants and mutterings seemed to grow louder, almost deafening, as my anxiety burned my insides. I desperately racked my brains. What do I do now? Should I throw myself on the floor? Start wailing? Start dancing? Or all of the above? I've always had a good degree of faith, but this 'faith' being practised around me was something I did not know nor want to be a part of. As I was swallowed up deeper in the group, drowning in their chants, the most genius idea came to me:

Broccoli, broccoli, cauliflower.

I began chanting it under my breath.

"Broccoli, broccoli cauliflower! Cauliflower," I chanted, clicking my tongue in my nervous spit. It was working! They were buying it! I couldn't quite believe that it had come to this: Me, chanting vegetables under my breath. But hey, it was getting me out of double science so damn right I kept doing it.

As far as they were concerned, I was healed. Cured. Blessed. Had THE GIFT. For me, since the day that genius idea was beamed into my head, it convinced me the kind of God I knew was a pretty cool dude.

Chapter 4 – The good, the bad and the ugly teachers

"School days are the happiest days of your life."

How many times did you hear that one when you were moaning about homework or uniforms? I hope for many of you this was true, and you look back on your school days with fond memories of great friends and inspirational teachers, who impacted your life in the most positive way. Maybe there was that one teacher you could run to and confide in about bullies? But what would you do if a teacher was the bully? Then there was literally nowhere to run, nowhere to hide. I experienced this first hand.

Let's, for the sake of argument (and me not wanting to be sued), call her "Mrs Wiles." She was the French and P.E. teacher. From day one she took an instant dislike to me, treating me completely differently to the rest of the class and coming down hard on me at every opportunity. To the boys she was patient, understanding and would talk to them as equals. The girls? Much the same but with a more condescending tone mixed in. I, however, was treated like a brain-dead, incompetent imbecile, supposedly rubbing her up the wrong way at every moment – whom she held a massive grudge against, as though there was some deep-rooted, unfinished business between us. As though I'd put fish guts through her cat flap and then maybe stole her cat and sold it to a travelling circus in the process. Who will ever know the reasons behind her behaviour towards me? But one thing's for sure, I became more and more fearful of her. Retreating into myself dramatically. Becoming increasingly quiet, nervous, head down, don't make eye contact, don't cough, don't even breathe and above all: SIT AT THE BACK! But she wouldn't let me get away with that.

"Sophie!" she'd snap, as we were all taking our seats.

"Here!" she'd command, tapping the desk right at the very front of class where she cowered over me constantly. Pointing out my mistakes on the page with her crooked finger (which strongly resembled the fingers of the evil old lady that handed Snow White the poison apple in Disney's adaptation). She'd humiliate me at every opportunity, asking me questions she knew I didn't know the answers to, shouting at me for 'not trying hard enough,' when I would say I didn't understand something.

I had a matching stationary set with various affirmations on the notepads and pens such as "I heart me"– "I'm a star"–or simply "Groovy girl!" and a cute cartoon illustration. From a young age, I had instilled in me by my mum the importance of self-love, self-belief, and the possibility that I could do, be, or achieve anything I wanted. Whatever that may be. As long as it made me happy and I wasn't hurting other people. For some reason this seemed to get Mrs Wiles seriously riled!

One particular day, she flipped at me again for not keeping up and getting yet another question completely wrong. "You're NOT listening!!" she screamed. "Everyone else can do it! Everyone else has got it! Where do you go in your head?" She violently tapped her temple with her crooked finger. "Are you at the ice rink? Are you whizzing round not paying attention?" She came and stooped over me, both hands leaning on my desk, coating me in a plume of her bad breath. (It was always vile.) "I'm telling you now, you are NOT a star and will never amount to anything or be anything with this attitude! Now pull your finger out and engage your brain!"

I glared up at her, and in that moment, I wished more than anything we were on the ice. I would drag her into the middle of the rink, leaving her there struggling like Bambi and proceed to skate rings around her. Coming dangerously close then aggressively stopping at the very last moment, spraying her with a snowplough stop and covering her with an icy blast... Before leaving her there, having no doubt fallen flat on her back as her clothes stuck to the ice. I'd show her...one day. Mark my words.

Things got worse when she'd physically come and find me hiding from her in the toilets on my lunch break. On days I wasn't even due to have a lesson with her, she'd come striding into the lunch hall with our French homework books under her arm. I knew she'd been marking them and was on the warpath. I abandoned my mini-Jaffa cakes and legged it into the toilets hoping she wouldn't see me, but in a school so small there was nowhere to escape. I locked the cubicle door, my heart pounding. It was silent and cold. And I waited. Alone. For all of about 30 seconds and then BANG! The old toilet door swung open as she proceeded to hammer on my cubicle door. Annoyingly there were only two cubicles and the other one was empty. I knew she had me. Sure enough, right on cue:

"I know you're in there!!" she screamed. "You can't hide from me! Open this door NOW!"

I didn't get a lunch break that day. Instead, I had to sit in the hall with Mrs Wiles as she stooped over me, coating me in the same foul breath, making me redo my French homework, yet again.

There was, however, one teacher that seemed to believe in me and that was Mr Riley, the music teacher. We only had that one subject a week with him and I wasn't particularly musical, but he was big on letting people be heard. He'd ask us questions as if we were real human beings and equals. He'd want to know our opinions and allowed us to voice our feelings. He made us think and question things, and didn't shoot us down for doing so, reminding us we all have a voice.

At the time, I was playing very basic violin. And before you ask – no, I wasn't particularly good and gave up as soon as the vibrato technique required me to cut my nails super short. I couldn't see myself continuing a hobby that required me to sacrifice a great manicure. While the other kids mimed on their guitars and recorders, Mr Riley set up a microphone stand in front of me to pick up the weak tones of my little violin so I could be heard. I was gutted when he left the school midway through my time there, but it was brilliant to see him go on to embark on the best midlife crisis, where he bought a motorbike, various fringed leather jackets and got his ear pierced. I always knew he was cool!

While I juggled feelings of rejection, isolation, self-doubt and hopelessness, among many other sensations school bombarded me with, I would find solace on the ice and anytime I stepped foot in the rink. I loved my coach, Mark, and I was excelling at the club competitions.

'The Monthly Medals,' as they were called, was the opportunity for us all to showcase our talents to the judges from all over the country and internationally, as well as our fellow peers and their respective pushy mums, who were high up in the Mother Mafia. It even gave the coaches chance to show off their pupils at their best, like a tiny dot, shining as they danced solo and uninterrupted across the huge, glossy ice pad. A welcome change from the busy practise sessions, where you would desperately try to not collide with anyone or get in anyone's way. You'd be right in thinking some people did this on purpose, though. Pupils and coaches alike, clearly side-eyeing you and nonchalantly gliding into your line of path.

Very quickly I was winning everything! I was beating people much older than me, who'd been skating twice as long – much to the annoyance of the other coaches, skaters and pushy mums. At one point, I was cleaning up in every category, bringing home an array of trophies made of heavy silver or beautiful ornate glass crystal. Standing on that top podium box, I felt so proud. I felt like a giant! I felt untouchable. Waking up on a dreary school morning seeing my whole bookshelf full of trophies glinting in the morning light made everything worthwhile. In the early days, I didn't really suffer with nerves and if I did, mum drummed them out of me by telling me how "This was my moment!' and "I was born to do this! Enjoy it!" –"Angels on your blades!" – "Sock it to 'em!" and more wonderful words to that effect. She was in it every step of the way with me. I didn't want anyone else there watching me. Only her and my coach.

My ultimate biggest fans though were her mum and dad – Nana and Poppa. Living two hours away in North Wales and being of quite ill health, they couldn't always make it to the rink. But mum would video tape all the action for them on an old camcorder. Oh, how I wish we had camera phones back then!

"Do it for Nana and Poppa!" Mum would say. And my God I wanted more than anything to make them proud. My heart would burst!

As well as doing everything humanly possible already to support me and my dream, mum didn't stop there. She took it upon herself to make all my competition dresses for me. This was a monumental task for anyone to take on. Especially if you weren't even a dressmaker and you were being judged not only on the skating but also your costume and how it interpreted the music and style of performance. The pressure was on! Many nights we had all gone to bed and mum was still up late into the night – slaving away over her old sewing machine at the kitchen table, praying it didn't give up on her. While other skater mums were competing against each other as to who paid the most to their dressmaker (anything from £400 to £500 upwards), my mum and I managed to cobble together the most amazing homemade creations! They really gave the posh kids a run for their money! I always felt a million dollars stepping out to compete when they announced my name over the crackly speakers. From an elaborate sketch design I scribbled onto a notepad, to her re-creation of it, with barely two weeks to go before an event, she always pulled it off.

Chapter 5 - Winning but Losing

One afternoon at the end of music class, I carefully lay my violin into its velvet-lined case. Mr Riley came over and started asking how my ice skating was going. I never spoke about it at school! I didn't want to sound big headed and, as I was already strongly disliked by the other girls and teachers alike, I didn't want to give them yet another reason to randomly hate me.

"Erm... I won two more competitions last night," I nervously mumbled, keeping my head down and avoiding all eye contact.

"Well congratulations!" he beamed. "That is just wonderful news. I bet you've got a lot of trophies now? How many is that?"

I'd amassed a lot. I knew I had, but I knew I couldn't say it. Although I resisted looking over, I could feel the other girls' ears prick up as they looked up from their usual huddle, death-staring me through the limp greasy hair that fell across their faces, or from behind thick, square glasses. Much like a pack of hyenas spotting a weak gazelle, knowing they were about to give it hell.

"Oh probably not that many yet, but I picked up a couple more small ones last night," I said, painfully modestly. It sounded better than, "Yeah I've got eight trophies now and a dozen medals, ten of which are gold and I'm on first-name terms with the guy at the local trophy engraving shop," which is what I really wanted to say.

"Wow! Would you bring them into school tomorrow for me? I would love to see them," he said so enthusiastically, with the biggest smile breaking through his wiry grey beard.

I thought about it all that night. It filled me with so much anxiety and I contemplated pretending I'd just forgotten to bring them in or, in return, hoping he'd forget he ever asked and never mention it again. But no. Why shouldn't I bring them in and show off my achievements? And more to the point, how sweet would it feel if Mrs Wiles saw me with them as I headed to Mr Riley's office? Cradling them in my arms as if they were Grammys! It would be worth it just to prove to her (and everyone else) that I was actually good at something. Weirdly, she already knew I was an amazing runner as she also taught P.E, but she would always refuse to acknowledge that I was a speed demon (for want of a better term!) across the fields.

She'd always shut me down with a condescending comment to the other students like, "When Sophie goes flying past you and overtakes you all, just ignore her".

I don't know why I bothered sometimes, but it was a great excuse to run away from her, very fast in the opposite direction.

The next morning, I nervously wrapped up my two most recent trophies in reams of kitchen roll, ready for their short but nail-biting voyage into school.

What I thought would be me casually introducing my latest silverware to an encouraging teacher, turned out to be him showcasing them to the whole school in Worship Assembly, making a proper announcement! He was documenting my achievements, as he called me up out of my seat to join him at the front and accept a round of applause. In more normal circumstances that would have been a real feather in my cap: a public acknowledgement of my achievements. I should have stood there feeling proud, listening to his congratulatory spiel, but all I kept thinking was, "Now I'm gonna get it..."

By the time first break rolled round, after (annoyingly) a full-length first subject as the Holy Spirit didn't 'move', I headed to the girls' toilet for a bit of a breather. All the hostility, snide side-glances and overall bad atmosphere I'd endured for the past hour and half had all got too much. I just needed to go in there, lock the door, maybe have a cry and then take several long, deep breaths. I used to do that a lot until a certain Mrs Wiles started following me in there to hunt me down. I'd often look down the side of the portacabin outside and wonder if I could fit down the gap and shimmy along with my back against the brick wall and hide there for a bit. No one would find me then. But they also might call the police and my mum, reporting me missing. I didn't want to cause any unnecessary concern, so I stuck with the first toilet cubicle on the left. Imagine the speed at which my heart dropped when I pushed that door open and was met with all the other girls having one of their huddles. It was enough to make anyone constipated. I shuffled past them to the mirror, pretending I was retying my hair, trying to act natural as though they hadn't all just fallen silent the moment I walked in on their conversation. Convinced they could hear my heartbeat thundering as loud as it was in my own ears, I attempted to make a quick exit.

"'Scuse me," I mumbled, reaching for the door. And then it started...

The girl nearest to it slammed her outstretched palm against the centre of the wooden door, preventing it from opening, while simultaneously sticking out her foot. Now what? I was trapped. The hurtful comments started flying at me; I felt like I was being speared from every direction.

"What you gonna win next? The Olympics?" one jeered.

I already felt like I was drowning and couldn't think of a comeback. I reached to pull the door again, but the next girl pressed it harder.

"Listen – we don't like you Sophie," another one began, a dig that surprisingly came from the most holy and quietest of this bitchy girl group. I never had her down for being the ringleader but here she was, running the show. It's hard to know what to say in the moment when you're in such an aggressive or stressful situation. Snappy comebacks would always flood into my head shortly afterwards, but never at the time when I needed them. I just remember saying, "I'm sorry! Can I go now?" and was then literally saved by the bell as it rang out, dispersing us all. I breathed again. I wish, looking back I'd learned what I've learned now: when someone is treating you badly, don't apologise for being you and blame yourself for their bad behaviour. YOU are not the problem. It's a shame it took me nearly 30 years to learn that.

As I fought to keep my head above water, the low blows continued to come... A new headteacher started and like any new boss, decided to come in and throw his weight around and change unnecessary things that didn't need fixing to justify his existence.

As my skating regime and training had got rapidly more serious over the first two years, school had agreed to let me train at the ice rink on the two mornings I would have had P.E., something very common amongst my fellow competitive skating peers. Rocking up to school after first break fresh from the rink, cheeks still ice-bitten and rosey from all the cold air rushing at me, I couldn't care less how bad my scores were in French or science... Although when I resorted to putting the word 'copper' as the answer for EVERYTHING in any science test, I actually ended up getting a one-off high score as it turned out to be the correct answer for the biggest, most longwinded, high scoring question in the test! Brilliant! I knew my strange logic would pay off one day. And it brought me more success than my previous idea of writing "Only smarties have the answer" as the answer for everything.

Striking this life balance made things seem more bearable. Yes, the girls were still bullies and poisoned dwarfs. Yes, Mrs Wiles was still on a daily mission to ruin my life and gassing me with her deadly breath, but at least I could skate two extra mornings a week! Then the next smack in the face came. And this one hurt more than most.

The headteacher decided it was no longer acceptable for me to train at the rink instead of P.E. I was so angry he didn't take my skating seriously, and to him my 'mere hobby' didn't warrant me the privilege of extra ice time. He clearly thought it was more beneficial for me to stand on a football pitch where I'd spend most of the lesson running away from the ball, and being shouted at by Mrs Wiles for, in my opinion, simply trying not to get injured so I could still skate. This was rich coming from him. Especially as his strange daughter faked a limp for years so she could get out of P.E and read her book instead. She became known as Harriet 'The Limp'. She was also irrationally terrified of bananas – particularly their skins. It became one of my favourite pastimes to purposefully walk past her with a banana skin while heading to the bin, and watch her runaway screaming as her limp mysteriously disappeared.

With no Mr Riley to fight my corner, and Mrs Wiles clearly having a part to play in this as phase five of her 'Ruin Sophie's life' mission, I was down to four short training sessions a week on the busiest ice times. It didn't cut it. I could see my performances and confidence suffering, but I had to make it work. Thankfully we only lived a 5-minute drive from the rink, and Mum would drop me there at every opportunity, then nip home and peel her potatoes for dinner. We were lucky to be so close by, as some skaters would travel an hour plus to get to their respective rinks or chosen coaches. Yes, Altrincham Ice Rink was an ancient, falling apart, rat-infested dive of a rink, but to me it was an ice palace. My sparkling white stage where no one could get me the moment I skated off into the centre.

Then the next blow came. The worst blow of all. News was announced that a popular housing developer had bought the ice rink and was set to knock it down within a matter of months, bulldozing it, replacing it with numerous matching town houses. It was like someone had ripped my heart out. Just two years into what was looking like a potentially glittering career, and something that was genuinely saving my life in many ways, would tragically be cut short before it had even properly begun. There was no hope and I felt like life was doomed. How would I and my family and coach figure our way out of this one?

From this day on, every day felt so much harder. So much more hopeless. As we tried to weigh up our options, it became apparent they were depressingly minimal. We had a choice of two other rinks, both equidistant to us in opposite directions, either towards Wales or Preston. Both were around a 2 hour round trip, traffic permitting. Realistically this would mean only being able to train at weekends. That wouldn't get me anywhere! But it would get my mum further into her overdraft, a glove box full of petrol receipts and the need for a more heavy-duty under-eye concealer.
But it wasn't up to us really. It all depended on where my coach would choose to go, and where any good coach goes, the pupil has to follow. Even if it means relocating.

Then came the next blow: Life blow No. 104. Or so it felt.

My coach announced he was moving to Texas. Fucking Texas!

"I may as well just pack it all in now!" I screamed in my head. I adored Coach Mark. He believed in me, saw something in me and plucked me from obscurity, igniting this ice dancing dream within me. I never felt anger or resentment towards him for his decision. He had to take care of himself, I knew this. He'd also recently struck up a relationship with one of the newly divorced hot skater mums, and planned on taking her with him to start a new life over there together. I couldn't blame him! I was heartbroken to see him go, but to this day it fills my heart with warmth to say he still lives out there, got married to his girl, had a baby with her, and truly found his happy ever after.

He suggested a couple of other coaches to me that I could train with during the last remaining weeks of the rink's existence, as he was leaving imminently. It was all so much to process along with all the other shit I was having to deal with in my school life. Yes, you've guessed it – that was not improving either. The ground may as well have just swallowed me up, dumping cold, wet earth on my head, and burying me in a pit of my own doom. Little did I know, another big change was about to come, and this one would change everything...

Chapter 6 – Throw me a lifeline

Health is wealth. A phrase so true but often overlooked. It's a phrase I'd often like to remind myself of and add other important factors: Mental health is wealth. Emotional health is wealth. Or spiritual health is wealth. Regardless of all the other external factors I was dealing with, ultimately the only thing that could stop me from skating was my own health. Or lack of it, as I was soon to learn.

The daily battle of school, the anxiety building in my lungs every lesson that I came into contact with Mrs Wiles. The constant put downs, the churning of my stomach, the hopelessness, the fear, the self-doubt. The bullying. My heart racing every time I pushed the girls' toilet door open. Breath shortening, head pounding, tension migraines, rapid weight loss, severe fatigue, insomnia or night terrors when I did eventually sleep... School was slowly destroying me. I became a shadow of my former self. My mum did all she could to fight my corner, going in to speak with Mrs Wiles or speak about the other girls' behaviour towards me. No matter how many times she confronted her, nothing changed. She would lie to my mum's face repeatedly. Being sickeningly sweet, assuring her she had my best interests at heart, and would allow me to work at my own pace, going easy on me, helping to build my confidence. When in reality she'd tear strips off me at every opportunity and continued to hunt me down in the girls' loo, where she'd find me there in that first cubical, a gibbering wreck.

I was a waif-like shell, with darker rings under my eyes than those left from a dripping coffee cup, staining a white surface.

Numerous trips to the doctors followed and I was referred to a specialist at the hospital. My parents were worried sick, concerned I had leukaemia, severe anaemia or

God knows what else. My brother, by the way, was coasting through life and school quite happily during all this, seemingly oblivious to my troubles and what was happening to me at school.

Then the day came for all my results from my numerous blood tests and scans. As we sat opposite the consultant, my mind raced as I tried to read his body language and gage was it good news or bad news? He hummed and hah'ed until he looked up and pulled his spectacles off his face.

"You have a very sick daughter on your hands, but none of this is physical," he sighed. "This is one very stressed little girl." I remember being relieved but also disappointed that there was nothing they could do for me. No quick fix pill or diet change. It was painfully obvious that the school environment was doing this to me and that was something that couldn't be changed. We'd tried EVERYTHING.

My default reaction on most days when I received any kind of bad, frustrating or confusing news, was to go for a long walk to mull it over and try to make sense of it. And that's exactly what we did. We headed to Dunham Massey, a stunning local National Trust park with roaming deer, majestic trees, picturesque lakes and beautiful secluded spots to sit and be. To think. To pray. To feel. Mum and I sat ourselves down on a huge old log as we recalled the day's events and tears of hopelessness fell from my eyes. It was right there in that moment that the most life changing decision to date was made.

Mum was taking me out of school and would educate me at home. I was 13 years old. I thought she was joking at first, but she was dead serious and was not prepared to stand by and watch me deteriorate anymore. My tears of hopelessness turned into sobs of relief. Disbelief. Joy and gratitude. We hugged so hard. Neither of us really knew the logistics or laws of home schooling at this point. That was something we'd come to learn and feel our way through. But one thing I knew for sure was Mum saved me that day.

From then on, I never went back. I never had to set foot in the building again! I had the best night's sleep in years and the next morning it was my parents that went into school, not me, and they told them the decision we'd made. I'd love to have been a fly buzzing around the wall, but merely picturing Mrs Wiles' face in my mind was enough. She would never breathe on me again; those girls would never trap me again. I could start to heal and grow without fear. I honestly believe had I stayed in such a damaging environment, where all the other teachers would say was, "We'll pray for you!" and not actually fix anything, I'd have become an anorexic goth, who sporadically self-harmed to gain some kind of control over the situation. I'm relieved to say it never came to that, and pink clothing remained firmly in my wardrobe and a healing smile began to show on my face.

Chapter 7 – Skater Boys

Over the coming weeks, I established a great routine, and it was a joy to see how much home schooling was suiting me. I was like a different person! A new and improved Sophie. My typical day began on the ice every morning, instead of in that old school hall chanting vegetables under my breath. My classmates became my fellow competitive skaters at the rink who were all mostly older than me, extremely driven and either past or present champions. I looked up to them all and was inspired by their work ethic and achievements on the daily. I'd be home before lunch and get stuck into various subjects including creative writing, meditating daily, even continuing violin for a while!

As my stress levels and anxiety reduced, it began to feel real sadness knowing that each trip to the rink was soon to be the last. It was slowly getting dismantled around us, with pieces of seating, signs, and the large clock gradually disappearing. I'd started training with two new coaches, both moving to opposite rinks. So, I knew whichever one I chose to continue with would determine which rink I'd soon be frequenting.

When the final day came before the rink's closure, I don't think I'd ever cried so much in my whole childhood as I did on that one Sunday. Everybody came for a final skate that day. People old and new, past and present. We all sobbed together as we stood in a giant circle holding hands crossed in front of our bodies, swaying as we wailed along to a distorted recording of Auld Lang Syne, blaring out through the old speakers. Even the cafe staff, skate hire lady, zamboni driver and members of the Mother Mafia, shuffled onto the ice in their shoes to join us. In that moment it didn't matter whether you were a skater, a coach, a grandparent, a

caretaker, competition judge or the slutty skater mum
sleeping her way through the teenage boys' hockey team.
Altrincham Ice Rink meant something to each and every one
of us, and held a special place in our hearts. We did all make
it off the ice eventually, as we helped one another to the
nearest open gate, vision blurred by our own tears. While we
piled into the sticky carpeted function room bar, a beige
spread of Iceland's finest had been put out for us to gorge
our sorrows. I'd always found it odd that ice rinks had bars,
as surely mixing blades and alcohol was never a good idea.
But I'm told they were mainly used for birthday parties,
functions or staff meetings. As it was my first and last time
in there, I preceded to binge on a not quite defrosted
blueberry cheesecake. I polished off the whole thing as
speeches were made and we reminisced over our times there.
I still to this day can't eat bargain supermarket frozen
cheesecake, but I'm probably not missing anything there.

I will always remember this poignant day so clearly.
How long we all hugged, the smell of the rubber floor as I
walked out those doors for the last time, my heart heavy. But
there wasn't time to dwell and wallow, as two days later (with
the taste of artificial blueberry still in my mouth every time I
burped), we were heading up and down the motorway testing
out which would become my new home rink. They were both
a step up from Altrincham: a larger ice pad and a much
higher standard of skating.
I was having some lessons with a guy who Mark knew. They
used to compete against one another and seemed pretty
similar, apart from the fact he was much chubbier and
increasingly unreliable.

Many times he wouldn't show up for lessons or would
be in the worst mood when he did. His star pupil was a
couple of years older than me and the most beautiful skater.
It was clear he was putting all his efforts into her, and it

later became rink knowledge that they were (highly controversially) more than just pupil and coach... He knew I knew, we all did. He became gradually sleazier in his behaviour towards me too. Plus, most days he'd turn up late or not at all. There's only so many times you can be let down by a coach after trekking 75 miles up the motorway for the privilege, before you begin to look elsewhere. Thankfully, as Blackburn Ice Arena was named a 'Centre of Excellence', there was no shortage of amazing coaches. It wasn't long before I was approached by the head coach and most well-known one of them all.

'Carol Bacon', as we'll call her, was a powerhouse of a coach with an eye for spotting new talent, pairing them up to produce unstoppable ice dance duos. She was a former Olympic competitor herself and above all, someone not to be messed with. When she invited me to join in with her Friday morning 7:00 a.m. group training session, I jumped at the chance. But my God was I unprepared! The other pupils were next level and I'd never been worked so hard in my life while on ice. The speed, the pace, the intensity of the session, the huge sound system blasting out high into the rafters around the arena – the atmosphere was electric! I won't lie, it was a shock to the system and at one point there was steam coming off my forehead, as my brow sweat evaporated off my hot head and hit the cold rink air. If this environment didn't produce champions, I don't know what would.

I was in awe of Carol's star couple, 'Daniel and Megan'. They had the coolest choreography I'd ever seen and had already won numerous championship titles. Things were good. My creepy ex-coach had moved rinks and I was loving every second training with Carol. Thriving off the motivational atmosphere every session, I started to see there was life after Altrincham Ice Rink after all.

Imagine my confusion when a mere couple of weeks later at the usual practise session, I see Daniel and Megan skating separately. Carol trained both of them individually and they didn't speak or skate near each other once. This seemed very odd and I was definitely not expecting what happened next. Carol skated over to me with Daniel and before I knew it, we were thrust together in dance hold, inches away from one another's face and being analysed and critiqued from every direction.

"I don't think you'll have trouble lifting her," Carol quipped. "There's more meat on a Turkey!" She smiled, with a glint in her eye.

Lifting me? I'd never been lifted by a skater boy before, or twirled around above anyone's head for that matter! Probably the nearest I got to that was being put on my dad's shoulders at age two. This was all very bizarre and exciting, but I couldn't help thinking what Megan was thinking! Was she staring this way? Crying? Giving me daggers? Or had she retreated to the locker rooms? I desperately didn't want to upset her, although we'd never properly spoken. Carol assured me everything was fine, but Daniel and Megan were no longer skating together and Carol wanted me to partner him instead. Wow. It wasn't even up for discussion, but I didn't need to think twice. I grabbed the opportunity with both hands and zero idea what I was actually getting myself into.

Within the hour there I was learning the very choreography I'd been admiring several days earlier. It felt like a dream! To think I was classed as a similar standard to Megan was a huge confidence boost.

Daniel didn't have much to say on the matter, or in general to be honest, but I put that down to him being a typical, moody 17-year-old boy with acne. Anyway, where the hell was Megan?! Right on cue she emerged from the changing rooms and stepped onto the ice with her soon-to-be new dance partner, out of nowhere! Wow. Okay. People move on and swap partners quickly here it would appear.

It's a strange dynamic – the one between skater boy and skater girl. One I'd quickly grow to strongly dislike. I didn't know at the time, but you were highly privileged if you got a dance partner. Or should I say "were selected" by said skater boy and coach. The ratio in this sport was WAY off. With at least 10 girls to every one guy, they had the pick of the bunch. They would hold try-outs where girls would flock from all over the country to the latest boy who'd just split from his current partner, just for a chance to be embraced in dance hold for half an hour and maybe try a few lifts to check you weren't too heavy. You'd be scrutinised within an inch of your life by the coach, skater boy and even his parents. Was the height difference too big or small? Were your hips in line? Did your body shapes, leg lines and skating styles match? Did your hair colours complement each other? Wealthier parents would also offer to pay for the boy's coaching (both on and off ice), ice time, costumes and even accommodation if required, to make their daughter a more desirable option regardless of skating ability. As the new potential couples danced around the ice being scrutinised, both sets of parents would sit together trying to make a good impression. Showing off their fanciest fur coats while the mother of the skater boy quizzed the poor girl's parents, machine gunning them with questions like "What's her star sign?" – "How tall is her father?" – "Who's your dressmaker?"

And it didn't stop there. Some girls, knowing they lacked skating ability, the necessary finances and/or morals, would go as far as offering sex on a side plate. The ultimate definition of prostituting your art, it would appear.

This spawned some very uneven couples and in later years, some very ugly babies. But let's be honest, how many teenage boys would say no? Having everything and more offered to you on a silver platter, girls throwing themselves at you, parents bribing you and an ego more stroked than a Persian cat. And thus, the skater boy was born.

Chapter 8 – Shut up and Put up

Obviously, I had no idea of all this at the time and had seemingly bypassed this whole contrived process. When I skipped out to the car park at the end of my session, I couldn't wait to wake up mum and tell her I'd been skating with a boy; doing lifts and was planning to compete this season in the Junior Dance category! I'd find her wrapped up in an old sleeping bag, napping with her driver's seat reclined as far as it would go. She didn't want to get involved in the Mother Mafia and I loved how un-pushy she was.
As long as I was still enjoying it, that was all that mattered to her, and she'd leave me to it, watching me skip off down the path, pulling my wheelie skating bag behind me.

The months that followed were intense and tensions were running high between me and Daniel. His attitude stank, and most mornings he clearly didn't want to be there. His mum, although not physically at the training sessions, was horrendously pushy and overly involved in every aspect of his and my life. Even down to what ointment he would put on his blisters. She had a shrine made for him in her living room, with every ice skating photo of him ever taken framed, old medals, certificates and his first pair of proper skating boots just hanging there in all their scuffed, smelly glory. I don't think she ever really warmed to me or my family. We were super laidback and not the typical skating family.

She was also in charge of our costumes and had the most horrendous taste, dressing her son in floaty shirts with frilly cuffs and collars and had him looking like Coco the Clown. Was it any wonder he didn't really want to be there? Looking back, he was a deeply troubled young man as most skater boys are, but what I still struggled to comprehend was how he took that out on me in the most twisted way...

While in lifts, he'd threatened to drop me if I asked him to do something slightly differently, or said he wasn't doing it right. And sometimes he would! He would literally just let go and I'd splat onto the ice like a sack of potatoes. When a guy is swinging you round by your ankles or holding you with one arm above his head, the number one thing you need is trust. I tried to put it out of my head or only work on certain things when I knew Carol was watching, in the hope he'd behave himself. But critiquing him or suggesting he try anything different was like poking a bear. What kind of sick person threatens to drop their partner in lifts and in some instances actually does?! Worryingly, things soon took an even more sadistic turn...

While working through our routines one day, Daniel was repeatedly messing up. It felt like he was doing it out of spite to annoy me or so we could keep stopping and have a breather. I nervously suggested we try it in a different way and go again. Out of nowhere he replied (eerily calmly), "I'll hit you."

"You'll hit me?" I echoed in my head, convinced I'd misheard him or was imagining things. I said nothing. A skater girl must 'know her place', I was beginning to learn: never talk back to the man, never question them and always let them decide everything. Above all, they were always right, and if you didn't like that, they'd replace you in a second.

We carried on and I said very little for the rest of the session. I felt so disconnected, almost zombie like, as fear and disbelief set in from the shock of his comment. We messed up again.

"I'll hit you," he muttered under his breath. I definitely was not imagining this now. My blood ran cold as the realisation set in that I was in dance hold, wrapped in the arms of a man who had said something so appalling to me. Twice.

"No you won't," I blurted out nervously, breaking away from him.

I chose not to say anything to anyone at the rink that day, but I was so relieved when the session was over, and I was safely on the 'girls only' side of the locker room. (Which, looking back, was a perverted set up with nothing to stop the boys peering round the corner of the lockers or simply wandering round).

I was noticeably quiet in the car on the way home. I didn't want mum to think I wasn't enjoying skating and all her efforts to get me there were for nothing. So I told her. And rightly so, she flipped. She made me promise that if he ever threatened that again, I'd get straight off the ice, take myself to the safety of the locker room and report it to Carol immediately. Carol was a rottweiler when she needed to be. Surely she'd have my back and put Daniel in his place for his disgusting comments?

Sure enough, the next morning it happened again over something and nothing. So small I can't even recall, but I immediately took myself off the ice. I pressed myself into the old fan heater in the changing room for all of 10 minutes, when suddenly the door flung open and Carol marched in, absolutely blazing, followed by Daniel. She dragged us both into the coach's room for a firm talking to. She tore strips off us both and got progressively louder and more red-faced as if she was a pan of boiling water, foaming and bubbling over. Hold on a minute. Why was I getting screamed at here when I'd not done anything wrong?

When she ordered us both back onto the ice, Daniel headed off first and I held back, somewhat paralysed by the uncalled for grilling I'd just received. As Carol held the door open for me, she lowered her tone to a whisper. She told me that this was just part and parcel of being in an ice dance partnership. This was the way the sport goes. If it meant I was one of the lucky ones to actually have a partner, I was going to have to suck it up and get used to it. It was a small sacrifice I'd have to make in order to win all those titles we'd been tipped for. (IF Daniel eventually pulled his finger out). I'd just have to grin and if possible, bear it.

"You don't upset the boys," she said boldly, and implied she'd put up with far worse in her skating partnerships, but it was worth it to make it to the World Championships. I shuffled out of that room with a heavy heart, knowing I was going to have one hell of a battle on my hands with this one, in more ways than one.

We continued training together and Daniel continued being an arse. Although once the choreography was set, he stopped dropping me in lifts and just got on with it, which was nice of him. We actually were getting quite good and the season was well underway, with various qualifying rounds competed in around the country, and all sights set firmly on the British Championships at the end of the year.

Every competition, test, or minor achievement I had, my grandad, Poppa, would put a congratulations card in the post to his 'Sophie Star', and he and Nana would have all the neighbours over to their bungalow on a North Wales retirement park. They'd celebrate with numerous bottles of champagne and gin, even if I didn't win. They kept every newspaper clipping and watched any competition or practise footage over and over again, until the video tape wouldn't play anymore. They really were my biggest fans and I was theirs. I'm heartbroken to say during this time my Poppa suddenly passed away. A huge shock to us all when he appeared so fit and healthy, and was the ultimate life and soul of the party. To ease the pain, Nana bought a Shih Tzu puppy called Oscar, who then tragically got attacked by a sheepdog on the beach and lost an eye at just six months old.

I'm pleased to report there was never a dog as resilient as "Oscar the one- eyed Shih Tzu," and he bounced back just as hyper as ever, humping everything that moved!

It was a big day for all of us, but most of all Nana, when she made the trip to come and watch one of our practise sessions. Her first time seeing me skate live in a while, and the first time seeing me skate with Daniel. The speed across the ice that gets lost when watching on camera and the sound of the blades cutting into the ice was electrifying for her, as she watched in awe and oozing with pride, wrapped up in several of her amazing crocheted blankets.

Danielle was charm personified as ever, barely acknowledging her and taking forever to even get on the ice. Surely he would be on his best behaviour with Mum and Nana watching, and actually try when it came to presentation or even crack a smile? But no. That day he portrayed his shittiest behaviour ever...

Considering my Nana had come all the way from Wales, was of such ill health and might never make it to the rink again, all she wanted was to see us perform our routine, with the music, start to finish. Even if other skaters got in our way or Daniel fell flat on his back again, she wouldn't mind. She'd been living for this day. As had I. But Daniel refused. He refused to put our music on, he refused to do any more than small snippets of the choreography that required the most minimal effort and no lifts. He appeared to take some weird pleasure in being so awkward and depriving my poor Nana of a simple performance run through. WHAT A BASTARD.

Annoyingly, Carol was on holiday, and I'd like to think if she'd have been there, she would have made him pull his finger out, but who knows. At that moment, when he snatched my hand and pulled me into dance hold to do nothing more than figure of eights, I hated him.

When I got home, I made a promise to myself: that I would keep going with him, putting up with his bullshit and putting myself in potential danger, just to make it to the British championships. Then after that, regardless of where we placed and even if we won and Daniel got a personality transplant, I would split up with him. Even if there were no other skater boys available, I'd figure it out. I knew I'd be severely going against the grain to dump a partner. Skater girls didn't do that. They were to shut up and put up and be grateful they ever got picked from the masses in the first place. But I also knew I would crawl through broken glass to make it to the British and perform on a stage as big as that. And I'd be damned if I'd let a dickhead like Daniel take that away from me.

Along with this ballsey, potentially foolish and soon to be frowned upon decision I had made to myself, I also made a 'Ditching Dan' countdown calendar, where I used brightly coloured pens, crossing off the days leading up to the championship, and highlighting the 'Dan free' days where I blissfully didn't have to come into contact with him. This was one of the many little things that helped me cope, even on the toughest of days.

Things got worse not better, but I kept going. Skating my heart out and skating for two, as I had to overcompensate for his lack of effort. I kept myself as fit and healthy as possible. But it wasn't just the girls that had to watch their weight, the boys did too, to a point. When Daniel's bottom started getting progressively bigger, we were relieved when his mum bought him a bike to cycle to the rink each morning. This was brilliant as it meant we didn't have to pick him up and drive him to the sessions (even less 'Dan Time'... Winning!) . It would keep him trim too, without me having to educate him on the fact sausage rolls weren't the best diet for an athlete. It's a shame his mood still stank. He was clearly a deeply unhappy young man. I was reminded of this yet again when his temper escalated after a session one morning, over God knows what. I can't remember. But what I do remember was him reaching new levels of aggression that day...

We were in the locker room, me on the girl's side, him on the boy's, as he was shouting and kicking off. I could feel his rage pouring over the tops of the lockers and flooding onto the benches.

"You can't come round here, I'm getting changed!" I feebly snapped back with. Lie. I was sitting on the bench drying my blades in actual fact, but it might at least keep him on his side for a few more minutes. But no. I'm a terrible liar and he could tell. He marched round to me, resembling an angry bull; red faced, imaginary steam coming out of his ears, the boils on his face looking like they might explode, shortly followed by his head. I leaped up and staggered back, my back against the wall, still clutching my ice boot. I froze, praying there was someone in the connecting coach's room and any second now they would fly out and protect me. Preferably the tallest and most thug-like male coach. But no. We were completely alone and Daniel knew it. I couldn't even hear his shouting words, I could only feel his aggression and hot anger radiating out of him, as the loud hiss of white noise grew in my ears and he lunged towards me. I just remember looking down at my ice boot in my hands and thinking "This has a blade on it, and if I have to use it for my protection, I will". Maybe like a woman taking off her stiletto and impaling it into a threatening man's shoulder, in a dark alleyway. Had it really come to this? Was all this really worth it for the British Championships? And my poor family, worried sick, begging me to call it a day with him? I came so close so many times.

Then – THANK GOD – someone flew into the locker room, causing Daniel to immediately back down and cower back into his imaginary cage. As if he were a dangerous creature, realising they weren't going to catch any prey today.

None of this was normal for most 13-year-old girls to deal with, but I believed I was destined for a far from normal life, and good things would come if I persevered through the bad times.

Chapter 9 – Farmyards and TV Cameras

I managed to balance out the intense weekdays on the ice with looney tunes, by getting myself a weekend job on a working organic farm. I'd always loved animals and nature, so this was perfect for me. Especially as it was open to the public as a "Fun Family Day Out," and Mum used to take my brother and me there when we were little. We'd bottle feed the lambs and enjoy the tractor rides and it probably fed my once-childhood ambition to be a farmer's wife. It held a lot of fond memories. I loved every second of working there, like having a laugh with kids my own age that had nothing to do with skating. Earning £2.55 an hour I felt like I was rich, but it also taught me the importance of working hard and saving some money so you could buy yourself nice things.

My proudest moment was saving up £100 (which took a while!) and taking myself into JD Sports, buying the very latest limited-edition Nike Shox- circa 2004! When I pulled out my little brown wage envelope and poured the contents onto the counter – fivers, pound coins and 50p's flying everywhere – the sales guy looked exasperated. I stood there beaming. I felt like the proudest girl in the world, the coolest kid at the rink.

Alongside my fun, light-hearted weekend job and fancy trainers, something else very unexpectedly cool happened and I still can't believe it. Like most things that you'll see transpire in my life.

My next-door neighbour was a cameraman for some of the biggest shows on TV and was good friends and colleagues with Becky Want, a local presenter, radio host and journalist. She was filming a new documentary show featuring people, places and happenings around the North West and, unbeknownst to me, I came up in conversation. Next thing we knew, the BBC were on the phone and wanting to make a documentary about me, following my training, unconventional lifestyle and schooling, and my journey to the British Championships! Wow. This was the most exciting life event to date. Proper TV? Me? My skating journey? Daniel would be sick! And even more deliciously, so would Mrs Wiles.

Within days there was a cameraman and producer in our driveway at 5 a.m., ready to film a typical morning in the life of little old me! They wanted to capture everything, and the first port of call was to capture me waking up, blurry eyed and reaching over to turn off my digital alarm clock. Teddy bear pyjamas and all! Not entirely what I'd expected as my TV debut but, hey, this must be what it's like being on one of those reality shows where there's a cameraman hiding in every aspect of your life. I flipping loved it! I felt like a star! Mum and I were miked up and they set up several cameras on the dashboard to film our car journey up the motorway. I almost forgot they were there until the time came to eat my breakfast and I proceeded to eat a jam smothered bagel and huge bowl of cereal as delicately as I could. But that wasn't the worst bit... I'd then always brush my teeth afterwards and spit out in my then empty cereal bowl. Lovely. No one wants to see that, surely, so I brushed my teeth in the most ladylike way possible and swallowed all the remnants! Have you ever swallowed your toothpaste – post brushing – instead of spitting out in the sink? Word of advice: DON'T EVER!

Hopping out of the car in my fancy trainers and skipping down the path into the ice rink, with my own film crew in tow was possibly the best feeling I've ever felt. All eyes locked on me as my fellow skaters nearly crashed, not looking where they were going, and the Mother Mafia craned their necks, not so subtly whispering to one another, "What the hell is going on with Sophie!" and more likely: "Why hasn't my child got a camera crew following them?" or "How can we get them on the show too?" My little camera crew were somewhat dumbfounded that my mum didn't come in to watch, as I imagined they were all set to portray her as 'the pushy mother' when in reality, she was whipping out her sleeping bag and bedding down in the car park with an Asda all-day breakfast sandwich.

Everyone wanted to be my friend that day. Doing all they could to talk to me, skate near me or prove they were better than me. Even Daniel played ball – until they mic'd him up too, and he proceeded to tell me how I was "doing it wrong again," while we danced round and all our audio was playing through the cameraman's headphones. A cheap shot, but I wouldn't have expected anything less from him.

The days that followed consisted of them filming every aspect of my life: the home schooling, the off-ice training, the ballroom and Latin dance classes, from Mum making my costumes and various pieces, to me chatting about my goals, dreams, friends, fears, the British championships and my relationship with Daniel.

"We're very different", I said with a diplomatic smile. Secretly I wished I could expose him as a complete and utter arse hole that actually hates skating and threatens to hit or drop his partners and, in some cases, actually does during lifts.

Life continued to take exciting turns as Olympic champion and Ice Dance legend Jayne Torvill turned up at the rink with award winning West End choreographer Matthew Bourne. They were scouting couples to cast in the Somerset House ice rink opening show and televised Christmas light switch-on in London in a matter of weeks. Daniel and I were cast, along with four other couples, as we embarked on the most amazing expedition to the Big Smoke, staying in the fanciest hotel, dress fittings, rehearsals, meeting celebrities and exploring the city! It was a very welcome change of scene and routine from the seriousness of training for the British, and was something new and exciting which we all thrived off. Especially having my little camera crew along with me! I was getting so used to being mic'd up, I'd completely forgotten what I was talking about at times. Like me and the other girls discussing how we all fancied skater boy Adam and "let's go for a wee now and sort our lip gloss." I was taken off-guard when cameraman Ed was waiting at the loo door to un-mic me before I went in, realising he'd heard everything we'd just been gossiping about. But still, I love the way I was constantly being filmed (although thankfully not in the loo). I'd merely get a phone call and Ed would leap into action, swarming around me, camera on shoulder, as if me answering my diamante encrusted Nokia and going "Hiya, Mum!" was the most ground-breaking footage he'd ever seen. I hoped that if I kept working hard, enjoying what I was doing and being nice to people, the future would hold a lot more of this for me...and maybe my name in lights!

When we all arrived back from our London adventure it was back down to business, as the British was only a couple of weeks away. But before that, we headed to Dumfries in Scotland to compete in the Scottish Championships. It was basically the British but held in Scotland, with all the same couples who you'd been competing against all season, and a great chance to showcase your Free Dance routine for the first time. It was also interesting to see what your opponents were dancing to, allowing you to make some last-minute changes yourself, and either be filled with confidence or the fear of God, depending what you were up against. The self-comparisons and judgmental thoughts in your head were the worst, and I was my own worst critic.

The day went in an absolute blur and I remember feeling the calmest I'd felt in a while before a competition. This resulted in us giving a technically perfect performance and an all-round 'clean skate'. As flowers and teddy bears rained on the ice and we took our bow and curtsy, I knew we'd nailed it! The scores came up and all our fellow teammates cheered as we quickly did the maths in our head and realised we'd won by a huge margin. My first championship title in the bag!

When we took to the podium for the winners presentations, we were awarded the most beautiful cut- glass trophy, and we not so subtly jostled over who was actually holding it for the pictures. (Think plastering a fixed smile on your face while muttering "MINE!' through gritted teeth.)

The following week my documentary aired. It was the most surreal thing: sitting in my own living room, watching myself on TV. And knowing this was being watched by so many others: Friends, family, skaters, rivals and most importantly, Mrs Wiles and hopefully the bullies. The sweet taste of victory, mixed with a massive 'up yours' and virtual middle finger. They edited it brilliantly and on the perfect cliff-hanger: presenter Becky, rink side, saying, "All roads lead to the British championships and could a gold medal be on the cards for Sophie?" as it cut to me zooming towards the camera and spraying it with a puff of ice in a sudden snowplough stop.

Chapter 10 – It Takes Two to Tango

The day finally came... The British Championships. The final day of my 'Ditching Dan' calendar and the culmination of 10 months of intense training and rehearsing. It all came down to this moment. Two performances. A mere 9 minutes to give it our all and not mess up. Worryingly it wasn't just up to me – even if I did the skate of my LIFE – if Daniel didn't pull it out of the bag too, we'd both get marked down.
We were at Nottingham ice arena, teeming with competitors, equally nervous parents and coaches from all across the country. The changing rooms were the worst. You'd constantly be gassed with hairspray, get shoved along the bench as other girls tried to commandeer the space with their bags, while getting daggers thrown at you from every direction. Above all: don't let your skates or your costume out of your sight. We all had little padlocks or zip locks on our costume bags as we'd all heard the horror stories of sabotage at championship finals. Girls' costumes getting slashed with penknives by members of the Mother Mafia, as they'd sickeningly frame their own daughter's friend for the crime, meaning they were unable to perform and would never speak to said friend again. A sinister ripple effect. Or then there were the ones who'd attack your actual skates: filling them with cut glass as you painfully slid your foot in after it was too late to realise, or bashing your blade in a door so it was bent and impossible to skate on. I tried to put all that out of my mind and find a quiet corner to warm up in.

As we stepped out onto the ice for our first performance, I could feel the nerves hanging in the air and tension in our hold. I skated my heart out and as we neared the end of our routine, I knew the feeling of relief was waiting for me, that we'd almost made it through with no mistakes. I spoke too soon, though. When the final bar of music played, Daniel tripped and went flying. Thankfully not taking me down with him, but still, I knew this would affect our marks overall. As I skated to the centre, I carried on and took my curtsy alone, while he lay flat on his back at the other end of the rink. We didn't skate off together which spoke volumes. I was livid. I just left him to it. He could either bow alone or, in my opinion, hang his head in shame and get off the ice at the nearest available exit.

Carol handed me my blade guards and we shuffled to the kiss 'n cry area to receive our scores. She said very little, but a calm and confident, "I think you'll be OK..."

OK? OK could mean a number of things: "It's OK. At least you looked good" or "It's OK, nobody died."

True, until she got her hands on Daniel, who eventually made it round to join us. He sat as far away from us as the bench would allow and didn't say a word. To our surprise and some kind of minor miracle, our scores were strong! Seemingly unaffected by Daniel's tumble and we were laying in 3rd place! Turned out his fall was a second after the last step of the dance, so wasn't taken into account in the marks. Thank God! This would mean all we had to do was pull a killer performance out of the bag and the championship title was still firmly in our reach! Or at the very least still a medal, if we maintained our place in the top three.

There was always an agonising few hours' wait before your next performance, where you didn't know what to do with yourself. Do you eat something? But not too much. Do you rehearse some lifts off ice? Or if like me, keep well away from your partner and go and eat some chocolate. We warmed up separately, then disappeared into our separate boy/girl changing rooms, before emerging in our sparkly outfits and gathering rinkside. Well, I did, but where was

Daniel? Carol and I stood scanning the arena as the penultimate couple before us finished their performance. Was he in the toilet? Having a word with himself maybe? Who knows? All I knew was that he needed to get his ass out here ASAP as it literally does take two to tango! I couldn't do this alone and the whole years' worth of blood, sweat and tears came down to this very moment.

"Right!", Carol snapped, blood boiling as she took off into the boys changing room. She found Daniel sat there entirely alone; boots laced, costume on, arms folded. Exuding one of his ultimate foul moods.

"What the hell do you think you're doing?!" Carol screamed.

"Not doin' it," he muttered bluntly. Was this his sick idea of the ultimate betrayal and self-sabotage? The ultimate way of getting one over on me and taking away my dream of a championship medal because he knew I physically needed his body on that ice in order to compete? I've said it before and I'll say it again: What a BASTARD! This was like a red rag to a bull for Carol. Let's not forget she had worked so hard to get us there too, and put up with all the shit.

She marched over, grabbed him by the scruff of the neck, pulled him to his feet, their faces inches apart and scowled through gritted teeth:
"Get yourself on that ice RIGHT NOW! I do not have time for this!"

Carol when she's mad was enough to put the fear of God in any man. He reluctantly agreed and I've never been so happy to see him emerging from a changing room.

It was the most emotion-filled performance I ever gave. Knowing this would make everything I've been through seem worth it, coupled with knowing that my dream could be waiting for me if the marks got lifted by the judges, and this was the last time Daniel would ever have his arms around

49

me; I gave it everything. But it wasn't to be. Daniel gave the most half-arsed performance of his life and we dropped to 4th place. Out of the medals and out of hope. I felt empty, cheated, defeated, like it had all been for nothing.

I never spoke to Daniel again after that final performance. There was a lot I could have said and wanted to say, but I would only be wasting my breath. Mum, on the other hand, didn't want to miss the opportunity to say the words she'd been waiting to say all year. She collared him in the corridor, came right into his face and said, "That is the last time you will EVER lay your hands on my daughter!"

He had no come back. He just huffed arrogantly and slid away from her intense glare and faded away into the distance. And that was the end.

It took me a good few weeks to lick my wounds and process everything I'd been through. The good and the bad. Before long, January would roll round and it would be the start of a new season, with new opportunities, new challenges and maybe a new partner...

Chapter 11 – Skater Girl 2.0

Getting back to skating on my own was the most amazing feeling ever. Freedom! I wasn't attached to another person and could dance, flow and curve in any direction I wanted. If I went down, it was purely on me. Sadly, that didn't last long because if you wanted to compete that season, you had to get your act together and get another partner.

This time it took me to Sheffield, where there was a newly available skater boy on the scene. He requested a try-out with me and when the boys say jump, you say, "How high?" (Please note: Don't you EVER apply this rule to life in the real world).

This particular skater boy trained at the second biggest ice arena in the country with one of the oldest and top coaches in the world. He was a lot smaller than Daniel and had a back problem, which he used as an excuse not to do certain lifts or implied I was too heavy. (I was tiny!)

Despite that, and his patronising tone with me and his sheer disappointment that I hadn't done ballet since the moment I left my mother's womb, he decided I was the girl he wanted to skate with.

I had mixed emotions but overall, I was excited and eager to see what we could achieve. I presumed there were ways of making it work and that we'd be splitting our training between Sheffield and Blackburn. But that's when (let's call him 'George') dropped his first bomb.

Apparently, he had terrible asthma and couldn't possibly train at Blackburn because it was too cold and damp and there was mould. Too cold? You're a bloody ice skater, mate! You've spent more than half your life in a freezing, rat-infested environment. I even developed Raynaud's disease in my fingers and toes (a precursor to arthritis where your extremities would turn numb and a yellowy white colour, as blood stopped flowing there due to freezing temperatures) as proof of my commitment to this sport! To this day, I refer to my condition as 'Alien hands' syndrome and quite enjoy freaking people out with it when I get cold, even though it can be very painful. I quickly realised this was going to be a very one-way street with no compromises...

This resulted in my mum driving me all the way to Sheffield before work, several mornings a week which nearly killed her, and then me staying with George's family the other days. (Which, I hated by the way.) They were the typical pushy, wealthy, overinvolved parents who recently moved house and their entire life up north from London so that little George could train at one of the best places with the best coach. Wow. I'd heard of people relocating for a great job but relocating your whole life so your mediocre, asthmatic skater boy son with a limiting back problem could skate every day, seemed a little excessive in my opinion.

I remember one night, his dad sitting me down and giving me a stern talking to when I didn't want to partake in their 'chippy tea' takeaway dinner, and was quite happy with my vegetarian ready meal Mum had packed for me.

"But there's not enough protein in it!" he lectured. "You need protein to make you a stronger skater."

Listen you idiot, when your son complains about my weight in lifts as much as he does, the last thing I'm going to allow myself is fish and chips! I screamed inside my head.

"I'll stick with my ready meal, thanks."

At least I knew the fat content in that – something I became unhealthily obsessed with, rigorously checking food labels before I consumed something. This resulted in me living on nothing but pasta and ketchup for several years, as I twigged there was virtually no fat in it, and it gave me energy.

I'm relieved to say this was a very short-lived partnership, competing in only one competition: the first qualifying round of the year in Coventry. It was doomed from the start when we had to stay in the biggest shithole of a Travelodge ever, in a tiny, dirty room that for whatever reason was hotter than a sauna! Poor Mum, who would normally sleep in the bath because she snored, woke up on the bathroom floor with her head against the toilet, because there was no bath. Grim!

It was the smallest and some would say less important round of the competitions, but it still meant a lot to me, and I always prided myself on making a good impression. But George and I just didn't look right together. As mum always said, "It looks like a beautiful swan with a small child clamped to her chest," when we skated together. Out of only four couples, we came an embarrassing 4th. I had never come last in my life! And to add insult to injury, it was Daniel and his new partner who came first. Ugh! That was one bad day at the office. I was so humiliated and Daniel was so smug. Carol was rightly disappointed and also pissed that she'd had zero input, as George had refused to train at Blackburn with her.

I so missed training with her and my other skating peers there. I let the dust settle over the weekend and on the following Tuesday, after much discussion with Carol, my family and myself, I made the most awkward and nerve wracking of phone calls. I rang George and told him I didn't want to skate with him anymore. He resisted my decision at first, making me feel so guilty, trying to twist my arm and give it another chance at the next competition. We were both good skaters but not good together. So that was that. I broke up with him over the phone. It was another highly controversial decision, and I was probably deemed the biggest renegade in the sport, having ditched two partners in three months. But I didn't care. I was so happy to be back skating at Blackburn and with Carol! I'd learned by now that nothing stays the same for long in skating, but what happened next still took me by surprise...

One of Carol's other star couples split, as the girl decided she'd had enough and wanted to go to university to become a vet. Good for her, I say! It was sad though, as she and her partner Jacob were the best of friends, always smiling and generally a lovely couple to train alongside. It hadn't even been a minute and Carol put Jacob and myself together. Partner number three in as many months! The other girls HATED me. But I'd been used to that since school.

Jacob was one of the nicest skater boys ever. He was a wonderfully expressive skater from the waist up, but worryingly his thin, bandy legs had a mind of their own. His long skinny arms made it feel as if I was dancing with 'spaghetti man' when we were in hold. We suffered several bad, unexpected falls in training. They'd come out of nowhere and SPLAT! One minute I'm upright, the next, my face and body was slammed against the ice, millimetres away from being smashed, teeth and all, leaving me breathless with quite literally the wind knocked out of my sails.

Mum came in to film us practising as Nana was desperate to see me with my new partner who, miraculously, wasn't a sadistic psychopath with the world's biggest chip on his shoulder. Or a small boy with a cotton-wool wrapped life, a big quiff and as much grit as the timidest of mice. This one sounded promising, right? But it wasn't relaxing watching us skate. It was far from smooth and the clipping of blades filled you with a sense of unease, like we were going down any minute. We usually did, and unfortunately it was me who'd cop for it, as his bandy legs would constantly knock into mine, wiping me off my feet instantly. Mum caught one of these awful crashes on camera, and it was helpful but also terrifying to seeing how easily and unintentionally he was taking my blades out from under me. Our bodies just didn't fit together. He always apologised for taking me down and it meant a lot that he owned up to it and acknowledged it, but I couldn't carry on skating in fear. I'd end up with no teeth, a cracked rib and probably a severed finger.

It was time to call it a day already. We didn't even make it to the stage of putting choreography together as we couldn't even get past the basics of gelling together! Carol was visibly exasperated by me at this stage, and my dumping-my-partner ways, but after a tough heart to heart and stern talking to from her, I stuck to my guns. I just wanted to skate on my own! To be fully free, with no one taking me down or having to rely so heavily on another human being. I wanted to do this myself. The only problem was, as a solo ice dancer there's only so far you can go. You can't compete internationally, and the British Solo Dance Championships is the pinnacle. Still a great achievement, and if I did well at that purely off my own merit, it could lead to great opportunities. Maybe I'd find the perfect partner, a role in an ice show or earning a fortune once I went into coaching. Either way, I knew I wanted to go it alone.

I'm so glad looking back that I followed my gut instinct. From then on I embarked on the happiest phase of my skating life so far. I had (nearly) complete creative control over my costumes, my music and my training schedule. I found the most atmospheric piece of music that had never been skated to before, and instantly it was the talk of the rink.

"Everyone is talking about your new free programme!" Carol grinned at the start of my lesson. "People are watching..." she added cryptically. Yes! They were, and this time they were only watching me!

As always, I worked my socks off all season, repeatedly medalling in the various qualifying rounds and feeling a million dollars in the very costumes I'd designed. Glistening like an aquamarine mermaid in an icy sea.

Once again though, it all came down to the main event. The most important date in the calendar, the one day to prove yourself: the Solo British Dance Championships. It came round in the blink of an eye, and having loved every minute of my first solo season on the circuit, my expectations were high, I'm not going to lie. I was the most confident I'd ever been and couldn't wait to get out there and show everyone what I could do. There were so many girls in my category but to me they didn't exist. Apart from one: Skylar Asakov. No, she wasn't Russian, but she'd been the favourite all season along with fellow rink teammate Amanda Ellison, a 'slightly larger' girl, you could say. The sad thing is, neither of them were particularly expressive or artistic, but they were both training at 'the rink of the moment', with the favourite coach of the moment (who actually was Russian).

Annoyingly this sport is savagely political, with the judges clearly favouring certain coaches and rinks and their pupils, from season to season. Even if they were embarrassingly mediocre, if they trained with the 'it' crowd and their coach was kissing up to the judges at every opportunity, they were halfway there. Irritatingly Skyler and Amanda had been the favourites all season. There was also a lot of backhanding going on, affairs and bribery. We all remember what happened at the 2002 Winter Olympics, when French judge Marie-Reine was "allegedly" bribed? I rest my case.

I chose not to let this bother me. I knew my free programme was stronger and more unique than both of theirs put together, and all I had to do was nail these performances and the best skater on the day would win. The first performance went like a dream. The build up to it was so relaxed now I didn't have another person's ego, moods or nerves to deal with. I simply had to manage my own and myself only. It felt wonderful. Stepping out onto that ice alone felt so powerful. I adored my costume, designed by me, made by mum, and all eyes were solely on me. I executed a perfect performance, despite being almost last on, and your warm-up skate starts to seem like a distant memory. But everything just clicked. I was lying in second place after my first skate with only Skylar bloody Asakov ahead of me. I could do this. I could beat her. I knew I was better! I just had to convince the judges to make me their new favourite.

During that awkward, nervous limbo time between performances, some news came to us that was quite honestly a kick in the teeth.

As well as my competitive career, I also had to have a Plan B as to what road to go down when I 'retired'. There were only really two options: go into shows or go into coaching. Call me crazy but shows never appealed to me. The thought of going to all these places, but never seeing the outside of the ice arena before moving on to your next country or city, and enduring the huge party culture that went with it, just didn't resonate with me in any way. Show skaters on tour go wild once they turn pro and aren't competing. After years of regimented routine, depriving yourself of most normal fun things, the cast members would hit the casinos, the clubs, the drink and the cigarettes hard after every show. Throwing themselves into the uni life they probably never had and performing severely hungover and queasy most nights. And yes, there was a lot of bed hopping, swapping partners, sleeping around and general sleaziness amongst the cast. Not to mention the hierarchy of Disney princes and princesses, understudies and chorus girls, both on and off the ice. I had no interest in alcohol, sleeping around or partying. And I'm sorry, but I'd not worked this hard all these years to dress up as Nemo, wave to terrified kids and hope my roommate who didn't even speak English, didn't bring yet another drunk, vomiting cast member back to our room to have sex with after the show. There was always the option of cruise ships... But imagine all the above going on and NOT being able to get off the boat! I'd been told it was like a five-star prison by other cruise ship skaters. So, with that said, I opted to do my coaching training. The rate per hour was good and I looked around at all the other coaches and their fancy fur-lined coats and sports cars and they appeared to have made a good life for themselves.

You couldn't coach and compete, and I had to wait till I was 18 to start my training but still, I had a plan! Like everything, it was thousands of pounds to study, and I'd been saving for YEARS to get anywhere near that amount on £2.55 an hour at the farm. So I applied for a scholarship. Only one skater per rink would be awarded this, but I was in with a good chance. The only other girl who also applied was the poshest, most privileged girl ever. She openly admitted she didn't want to coach as her career, she was purely doing it because it would look good on her uni application. Her dad was some kind of Army Commander or Sergeant Major, and they would regularly holiday on private islands in Mauritius. She didn't need the money and clearly just enjoyed this sport as a hobby. And that's fine! Then there was me, on the other hand: my family sacrificing everything including the family holiday, Mum deeply into her overdraft, home educated, Scottish Champion, working on the farm and dedicating every other waking hour of my life to ice skating! Plus, I had a documentary made about me. Surely there was no contest?

"I need to tell you something," Mum whispered, as she came down from chatting to one of the skater grans on the higher seats. The skater grans and grandads were the good guys, and often the first to hear the latest news, but selective of whom they chose to tell.

"Harriet Clements has been chosen for the scholarship," she blurted out. I screwed up my face in confusion as if to say, "Are they mental?" Did they even read my application? Probably. But it's amazing what friends in high places can get you. Or an application possibly written in gold leaf and a Royal Crest at the top of the thickest of paper.

I was so much more worthy of this scholarship than she, and the injustice of it all burned sourly in my mouth. But I had to shelve it. I couldn't let it get to me or knock me off balance. Save it for the car ride home! I was really glad Mum told me, because my God, was I fired up for my main performance. I'll show them!

Carol knew there was a lot at stake here. Keen to keep me in the right headspace, she took me down to the warm-up area super early. The category before me hadn't even finished yet but there I was, warming up rinkside, trying to get in and stay in my zone. As I watched all the other girl's routines before me, it became more of a struggle not to become nervous or distracted. But at least I was here and ready to go.

When my time finally came, I felt like I'd waited an eternity to step on to that ice. I could sense that a usually calm and icy cool Carol was a little jittery herself. She grabbed my hands over the barrier and squeezed them tight, looking in my eyes and giving me the nod as my name was called over the tannoy.

The whole performance felt like slow motion to me. Like I was hovering above my own body as a spiritual being looking down on myself giving the performance of my life, eyeballing the judges and oozing confidence like a proud guardian angel. All of a sudden, I was back in my own body, taking my curtsy, drinking the applause in, hoping I'd done enough.

The scores were close and there were still a few girls left to skate, one of whom was Amanda Ellison, dancing to the Chicago musical theme. How many times had THAT been done? If you're not in the skating world you might be unaware, but believe me, it's been done to death. I knew I'd be streets ahead of her in the originality vote. She could kick her leg up very high for a larger girl, though, it had to be said. I always chose not to try to calculate the scores in my head as they went along. I'd rather wait until I see it in writing – on that official result sheet stuck on the Perspex plastic lining of the rink's barriers by the oldest looking stooped-over man, who had usually been an official mediator for the past 108 years. We'd all crowd round to see the final placings, nearly stampeding the poor man and his Blu Tack. That's usually how it goes. But this time I held back. Before the official results were posted, the skater gran my mum had been chatting to had been keeping track of the numbers like she was at the Friday night bingo. We knew the scores were close and Mum sneaked up to her, bursting with nerves and stifling potential euphoria.

"Sandra! Psst! What do you reckon? Has she done it?"

Sandra shook her head solemnly.

"Third", she replied painfully. Third? How could she have dropped a place on that performance and "Who needs to be strangled out of the judges?" were many things possibly going through my mum's head.

"Third? Who was second then?" she whispered.

"Amanda Ellison," Sandra replied. At that point, Mum took off to find Carol and me in the corridor. Carol was anticipating the news, having roughly done the maths in her head, but she couldn't break it to me. Mum did.

"I'll give you a minute", Carol said calmly, as she went off for a moment of reflection herself, leaving me and mum to just look at each other. Lost for words but saying a thousand of them at the same time. I felt the sinking feeling of disappointment, as all the adrenaline and hopefulness flooded out of my body through my feet, gluing me to the floor in a gloomy daze. A tiny shred of me wanted to see what the official sheet of paper said, in case there'd been a complete miscalculation, and this was all a really bad Chinese whisper. But right on cue, Carol returned shaking her head in dismay. The final placings were up and my worst fears were confirmed: third place. Skylar Asakov in first, and pipped to second by Amanda and her ungainly high kick.

It confirmed the shitty reality of the politics and favouritism in the sport. The judges 'favourites' based on a number of seemingly unnecessary factors. Carol did her best to sugar-coat it and soften the blow but it was still like being slapped repeatedly. She was wasting her breath at this moment, but I appreciated that she tried.

What sunk in more was when a fellow Blackburn coach came over to console me. I loved his honest and frank Liverpool tone.

"I know Sophie, it's shite isn't it? You were by far the best skater on the day but sadly that's not who wins in this game. You've gotta wait your 'turn' as this is only your first solo season. You've gotta do your time... You might win it next year and not skate as well as you did today! Or maybe Blackburn Ice arena, and me and Carol will be the favoured coaches next season? But keep your chin up, Soph, everyone is saying you should have won today. Better to be like that than everyone saying you shouldn't have. Anyway, safe journey home, yeah?" And off he wandered.

"Thank you, Craig – lovely words there, appreciate it!" Carol said as she replied for all three of us. I still couldn't speak but so appreciated hearing that from a completely unbiased source. While Carol got swept away and preoccupied with her other skaters, Mum and I stood there paralysed, absorbing it all in silence. I hated this sport in that moment. And I wasn't much of a fan of life in general right then either. It was then that something profound came into my head and heart out of nowhere. I felt it so strong, and as crazy as it sounded, I came out and said it:

"Something really good's going to happen," I proclaimed with such sureness and belief. "Something really good is going to happen!"

Chapter 12 – Canadian Curveball

The following days and weeks felt pretty bleak. I've never been so disappointed with a medal in my entire life. But after every disappointment, there comes that moment when you have to get back on the ice. Because if you don't do it then, you never will. You skate around aimlessly, trying to keep your legs well-oiled and maybe contemplate thinking about ideas for your next routine. I was severely uninspired and bitter, but it was around this time that life threw me a delightful curveball: an invitation to join a training summer camp in Canada.

I had a chance conversation in the locker room with championship- winning pairs couple, Adam and Sarah, where they were telling me of their plans to train in Barrie, Ontario (not far from Toronto), for eight weeks. It resulted in Adam saying, "Why don't you join us?"

My brain was running pretty slow, still stuck on the thought of the bronze medal that should've been gold.

"You might nab yourself a Canadian dance partner! And I'm sure you could stay with the family we're staying with... You could share a room with Sarah," he continued.

Sarah never spoke but smiled her big, trademark gummy smile. Adam was right. Why shoudn't I join them? I honestly couldn't think of a reason not to, and this could be exactly what I needed to get me out of the stagnant, post-competition state I'd found myself in.

Adam was a bit older and could see I'd been hard done by and naturally struggling with motivation. I also think he felt sorry for me. I decided I'd take his pity! There was no time to lose, though, as they were set to leave in two weeks and there was a lot to organise before then. Financially, it was going to be a big hit for Mum and Dad but staying with the family friends of Adam's really helped. They were used to having skaters lodging with them from all over the world and the mum would even provide a daily packed lunch for us to take to training sessions each day. How lovely! Although it turned out to consist of three-day old Mac and cheese leftovers that would come out in one brick-like chunk from the Tupperware. Not that it mattered to Sarah, as I think she had a slight eating disorder and would live on mini Milky Way bars.

This trip was exactly what I needed. A new challenge, new motivation and the chance to get the hell out of this country! I'd always dreamed of going to America or Canada and suddenly here I was, sat in a three across, the biggest plane I'd ever been on, next to Adam and Sarah and their matching tracksuits.

The house, which would be our home for next eight weeks, was in a beautiful cul-de-sac backing onto a lake in a rather affluent area. It felt weird at first. Two weeks ago I was sitting in the grotty Blackburn locker room, talking about a potential Canada training trip, and suddenly here I was eating bagels in this family's kitchen that I didn't even know. We carbed up and got an early night, ready for the first day of camp tomorrow. I was on a different timetable to Sarah and Adam as they were a couple and I was solo, but I assumed I'd meet loads of other solo teenage dancers and hopefully make new friends.

Unfortunately, Solo Ice Dance wasn't even a category in Canada, so when I rocked up, the coaches had no idea what to do with me or where to put me. I still to this day don't understand their logic but for some reason they put me with the kids... the 2- to 12-year-olds! Which meant only two hours of ice time a day because, let's face it, kids have a short attention span and the last half hour of every session was spent playing games. Here I was, a 15-year-old champion ice skater, having flown halfway around the world to be put in a glorified on-ice creche and summer school. There's no way I could cope with seven weeks of this! I got more ice time back home and didn't have to deal with idiotic questions like, "So you're a solo dancer? How do you lift yourself then?" Or the bitchy cheerleader types in the changing room, saying loudly, "Who's that fuzzy-haired girl?" pointing at me as they mocked my wispy cowlick baby hairs framing my face, which I still hate to this day.

I had a lot of time to kill while waiting for Adam and Sarah to finish their jam-packed itinerary on the many other adjacent ice pads and dance studios, so I spent a lot of time sat in McDonald's, eating fruit bags, or going in search of smoothie bars and discrete bins to ditch my solidified packed lunch. After nearly 10 days of doing the above and not much else, it became apparent that this was NOT going to work for me, and spending another six weeks doing this would be the biggest waste of time ever. I was skating half as much as I did back home and was coming dangerously close to screaming at the irritating kids getting in my way at the overcrowded sessions. After some tough deliberations and expensive phone calls home, Mum, Dad and myself all agreed I was to come home and they arranged a flight back for me the following week. I was gutted the trip hadn't turned out the way I'd hoped and there was still so much left I wanted to see and do, like Niagara Falls and the outside of an ice rink. So, on my last weekend, Sarah and I decided to get out there and explore! I managed to persuade Jenny, who was looking after us to let us take the coach to Toronto for the day. She reluctantly agreed and I assured her I was a sensible and competent 15-year-old girl, wise beyond my years. Maybe a slight exaggeration...

When she dropped us off at the giant bus terminal, we decided to try to convince the ticket officer we were both in fact 11-years-old so we could get a child's ticket and pay only $5 instead of $30. Sarah never spoke anyway and only flashed her gums nervously, so it was always down to me to do all the talking. I figured looking all innocent and putting on a squeaky voice would convince him. It did! – although he responded by saying we needed a parent or guardian to be travelling with us, and swiftly told us to step aside to ring our mums as he served the next customer. Shit. What do we do now? This was the only bus and it leaves in 15 minutes. I desperately wanted to see Toronto and the clock was ticking while he glared at us through the glass. Honesty is always the best policy Sophie, and there was nothing else for it than to approach the dirty glass and come clean.

"I'm so sorry to do this but we are in fact 15. We don't have a lot of money and thought we could save ourselves a few dollars by lying about our age to get a child's ticket," I began. He glared at us, looking highly unimpressed and occasionally blinking. I was waiting for him to say something in return, but he didn't. Naturally, I started nervously waffling and filling in his silence.

"Lying isn't big or clever," I preached on his behalf. "And I go home to England on Tuesday and I would love nothing more than the opportunity to see Toronto, if you would just let us on the bus please?!" I stopped. Sarah was about as much help as a chocolate teapot. He sighed and gave his eyes the biggest roll and issued us our tickets. I thanked him profusely for both of us and scuttled off to the bus, then cowered in my seat with sheer embarrassment.

Toronto was so cool, and it was worth every agonising second of conversing with the ticket officer. We hit the hugest mall, got pizza, got our make-up done and I snapped pictures of everything on my disposable camera. We got a bit carried away and stupidly missed our bus home which required us to purchase another one-way ticket back to Barrie. This wasn't a problem for Sarah; she didn't appear to have a voice box but she was sensible and, unlike me, hadn't spent all her money on lip gloss and watermelon from the street vendor. I kicked myself as I knew I still had six weeks' worth of spending money in my suitcase back at the house, which my mum had budgeted for me in clearly marked weekly envelopes and instructions when to open them. Damn. I had no way of getting cash and Sarah only had $10 she could lend me. I'm still ashamed to this day that I had to do this, but I decided to approach friendly looking people on the street and beg for money. Thankfully I only had to stop one person and she obliged, although clearly exasperated with me and my incompetence of spending all my cash on kerbside watermelon. She had two daughters with her, though, and I imagine she thought what she would do if one of them were in my situation.

We boarded the bus and once again I melted into my seat with shame. Overall, it was still an amazing day full of adventures and learning experiences. But had I learned anything where money management was concerned? Clearly not, as when we got back to the house, I tore open all my envelopes of cash including one marked "FOR EMERGENCIES ONLY!" with the thought process of "Shit! I leave next week and I still have all these dollars to spend! I'd better get shopping and living!" Not for a second thinking I could take them home, unopened and convert them back to British pounds. God no. That sort of logic didn't even factor into my teenage pea brain, with my frontal lobe still on a high from the adventures of the day and new lip gloss. As most girls will know if they're old enough, from 2003 to around 2010, lip gloss was life! Even though your hair did constantly stick to it. I still relish the non-sticky matte lipstick movement that came in later years, fuelled by Kylie Jenner. Still, in those remaining days I did more shopping than skating, more eating than dance exercises and genuinely thought I was doing the right thing; by using up my dollars before coming home, I was helping everyone!

Sarah and I went to Canada's Wonderland theme park and spent all day repeatedly riding (at the time) the world's biggest, tallest and fastest wooden roller coaster. I was splashing cash on extortionately priced theme park food and continuously paying to play the arcade games until I eventually won the giant, pink, fluffy monkey with Velcro hands that I did not need. We kept going round again on rides with this giant monkey around my neck, well into the sunset, completely losing track of time and not being at our pickup point for our temporary skater mum to pick us up before it got dark. Unbeknownst to us, she was freaking out and sent the Park Rangers to find us. This probably wasn't hard as I stuck out like a sore thumb: an overexcited British tourist carrying a tub of candy floss and a giant monkey, while wearing a souvenir cap and hoody.

"Are you Sophie and Sarah?" the Ranger questioned us, as he pulled up to us on a golf buggy.

"Erm, yeah. Do we have to leave?" I squeaked.

"Yes! There's a very worried guardian waiting to collect you and you're not there where you arranged. Hop on and I'll take you to the exit."

Sarah and I looked at one another and had a fit of giggles, as we zipped through the park on his golf buggy.

I'm sad to say I didn't make it to Niagara Falls but it was probably for the best, as the way I was going I probably would have booked myself on a helicopter tour of it.

When I arrived home, it was somewhat embarrassing explaining what a waste of time the training camp was, and that my biggest achievements were the ability to spend vast amounts of money in a short space of time, and talk my way out of many sticky situations! Also, quite commendably, my ability to navigate my way around a huge foreign airport and get on the right plane. Flying long-haul alone as a minor made me realise how much I love to travel and wanted to do a lot more of this in future. Small victories aside, my parents were absolutely horrified I'd not brought any of my spending money back with me. I think the veins on my dad's neck would have popped out less had this been a result of me being mugged, rather than me just having gone on a lottery-winning style shopping spree and day trips. They've never let me live it down to this day and I'm happy to say I did learn from it, and vowed to be super smart and sensible with my finances in future. I'm still a big saver when I can be, and I recommend you do the same where possible. Even if it's just substituting watermelon for cantaloupe.

Chapter 13 – You Couldn't Write This

I came back down to earth with a bump, once I realised I was back to square one, skating aimlessly around. The disappointment began creeping in that Canada wasn't all I hoped it would be, and the only thing that benefited from it was my wardrobe. I had to get back to business. I had to find my motivation, and maybe start entertaining the idea of searching for new music to skate to.

I'm not even sure I got that far, when late one night we received a vague and rushed message from Carol. She'd been contacted by a TV production company who were looking to make a show about an ice rink. They were looking for skaters to cast and it would involve some acting as well. They were coming to the rink tomorrow to audition us girls. That was all we knew, as she hastily crashed the phone down, knowing it was now 10 p.m. and I suddenly had a very big day tomorrow, it appeared.

Considering the life events and crushing lows I'd felt over the recent weeks, I didn't get my hopes up. Knowing my luck, Skylar Asakov's dad was probably funding it and would cast me as the role of a tree, which did actually happen to a skating friend who played exactly that in the movie Blades of Glory, and was proudly credited "tree" as the credits rolled. But hey ho, I went in that morning with zero expectations, completely blind and hoping I at least would get a fair shot. At least I was semi used to TV crews.

As I skated round, keeping one eye on the entrance, I spotted them as soon as they arrived. Three of them. They shuffled around to the seating at the opposite side, where they began watching, whipping out their note pads and looking painfully out of place with a job to do. One of the ladies was aggressively chewing her biro, then frowning and pointing at us with it. I was used to being scrutinised and pointed at, so thought I might as well put on a bit of a show. Carol put my music on and I danced my routine from the British, which felt oddly cathartic to do it again but in a very different scenario.

My music ended and it was as if they'd seen enough. Maybe they loved it, maybe they hated it; either way, they were heading to the function room where we all met them off ice. We sat in a long line, where we were pointed at, scribbled about and then, one at a time, called into a separate room. It was a bit weird but also very cool, as we were suddenly all handed a script to read through and then recite once we got in there. I'd done very minimal drama at school as after Year 8 we didn't get the privilege. They had obviously decided science was more important. I'd disagree, as the ability to act happy when you're dying inside or dealing with an idiot was one I'd used far more than the ability to make a baking soda volcano erupt.

All the other girls we're messing about and taking the piss of the whole situation as if the novelty of being in the sticky carpeted function room was all too much. I went very quiet, reading through the lines over and over in my head, trying to prepare myself for all eventualities. There were two girls in the scene: one privileged, not arsed about skating and only doing it because her mum had promised her a boob job if she did well at her next competition. And she would regularly get caught with hockey boys in the toilet cubicles. (Funny!) The other, was a talented and quiet girl who adored skating but couldn't really afford it and was coached by her mum! The girls were best friends despite being competitors, and I loved the dynamic between them.

When they called me into the room, they all introduced themselves and, despite all their official and showbiz-sounding job titles, like 'Casting Director' or 'Executive Producer', they were all really lovely. They seemed to appreciate the fact we were all new to this and tried to and put us at ease.

They asked me to read for the part of Trisha, the nice girl. I was definitely more similar to her! The camera pointed towards me, blinking in my face, and Director Sarah read the opposite part with me, still managing to chew her biro in between lines. I was in and out pretty fast but told to wait with the other girls, as they then started bringing us in in pairs. The whole thing felt like a really fun acting experience and just what I needed to shake off the stagnant, bitter feelings of the British. So, imagine my surprise when they announced the four girls they were taking through to the next round to audition at BBC headquarters, and I was one of them! I was buzzing, of course, but trying not to get my hopes up, as they were set to audition girls at all the rinks up and down the country.

"Congratulations Sophie," said one of my fellow skaters, bitterly, when we emerged from the dingey, cold building. You can imagine the level of bitchiness and jealousy going on already towards us chosen four. Mother Mafia members were literally collaring the TV team in the car park, who were quickly departing to escape their obsessive, pushy behaviour.

I'd made it through the first round and wasn't yet traumatised. I was filled with a newfound sense of excitement. It was hard to not let the 'What If' thoughts creep in. What if I got the role? What if I ended up on the show? What if I got a bit famous? What if I ended up being an actress instead of a skater? In the words of Coldplay, I went to bed that night with "a head full of dreams."

There is no better energy than excitement for me. I could be awake for two days straight but when something exciting was unfolding in life, the thrill of my waking hours far outweighed the dreams I conjured up in my sleep. Life was potentially throwing me one massive curveball and I was thriving on it. Phone calls, emails, letters followed, containing scripts and audition times and whereabouts.

The day I first walked into the BBC headquarters and signed that visitor's register for my audition, I felt like I just walked into NASA! There were screens everywhere, displaying various studios on TV shows. A radio station played out across reception, which featured a spaceship-like welcome desk, and behind it a wall of enormous world clocks, because we all need to know exactly what time it is in Sydney or Shanghai! I was given a visitor's pass to clip on to my jeans, that I am proud to say I never handed back afterwards, and it now lives in my bedroom's memory drawer. Along with a variety of unusual objects and achievements such as old VIP wristbands and the mouthpiece from the first time I was breathalysed. (As I said at the beginning, things did get pretty weird at times.)

I was super early because I got the tram into the city centre and it's the most unreliable thing ever, but cheaper than parking or getting a bus lane fine. I sat nervously in awe, my eyes flickering everywhere, my ears tuning into the shows and channels I was exposed to. Other girls began arriving. I didn't recognise any of them, but you could tell they were skaters from their perfect balletic figures and pushy mums by their sides.

Suddenly I was snapped out of my overanalysing daydream by the cheeriest runner ever, who was sent down to collect us all. The poor girl got to experience my disgustingly sweaty handshake and proceeded to make the smallest of small talk with us in the lift on the way up.

"So you're all ice skaters then?!"

"No," piped up one girl. "I'm an actress," she said, glaring at us mere mortals.

Considering the playing age was anything from 14 to 18, she was definitely pushing 26. But with age came confidence, clearly.

After what felt like the longest lift ride ever – I half expected to step out on the moon – a spine-tingling sense of excitement, wonder and nerves shot through my body.

"If you'd all like to take a seat here and we'll call you in individually." The assistant smiled. My eyes darted round again to assess my new surroundings, this time it was a long corridor with pictures of broadcasting and acting legends lining the walls. A red box displayed "On Air" lights above certain doors, sporadically lighting up. I was drinking it all in. The fact I was even in this building was flipping amazing and whatever happened, I figured I'd steal the visitor's pass to prove it!

When they called me in, I was met with the same three people as before, an already-set-up camera and another lady also with many biros. I was noticing a theme here. They seemed genuinely pleased to see me again, unless that was more me just being ecstatic to be there! It went in a blur from the moment they hit "record" and I was punching the air in my head for remembering all my lines perfectly and not fluffing once. I was then taken back outside to the waiting area before being called in once more. They appeared to be pairing us up to see our chemistry on camera. Naturally, I thought everyone else was way more capable, pretty, confident and overall better than me, in most ways, but I could at least put all this down to experience regardless of the outcome.

As we were all placed in the holding area for the final time, after a short but painfully long feeling wait, Director Sarah emerged with the next nugget of news.

"OK girls, thank you so much for coming today. We've decided to only take three of you through to the next stage. Those three are: Sophie, Jade and Olivia. Congratulations, you three, we'll be in touch with what's happening next. You're all free to leave now and sign out at reception." She smiled, oozing professionalism and an air of cool, then quickly headed off back down the corridor before the unlucky few (and their mums) could kick off. It was like a hit-and-run: deliver the necessary information then leave. Some of us were frozen in time as we digested the news and what it meant to us. Others were already leaving, reaching for their bags, cursing under their breath and almost at the lift doors. I needed a moment. Without realising it, a dazed and mesmerised smile had spread across my face and my heart raced with excitement.

"Well, that was a bloody waste of time! Come on, let's get out of here," hissed one of the skater mums, snapping me out of my dreamy thoughts. I congratulated the other two girls and took my time heading back to reception, diving into the ladies' loo on the way, not wanting to leave the exciting bubble of this building. I pushed my way out through the turnstile, taking my visitor's pass as a souvenir with me. I pretty much levitated my way to the tram stop while on the phone to mum, echoing her high-pitched squeals as I shared the good news. But I wasn't out of the woods yet. Okay I was down to the final three, but all of this could end tomorrow. If I didn't actually get the role, all of this will have been nothing more than a fun day out to BBC headquarters, a taste of what an auditioning actress life might be like and a stolen pass to keep in my memories drawer. I've come so close but it could turn out to be one of those things that nearly happened. Like when I nearly won the British. Twice.

The next few days that followed I couldn't think or talk about anything else. I couldn't dream about anything else. This was opening up my mind to the idea that I could be so much more than just a skater. There's so much more I could pursue, I realised, and I should absolutely dare myself to dream about it. Even if I didn't share those ideas with others, I could still at least open my heart to them.

Every morning at the rink that followed, Carol, other skaters and even people that never spoke to me were suddenly asking, "Any news?" –"Have you heard?" – "So did you get the part or what?"

It made me think I should definitely NOT tell people when I'm doing my driving test. Imagine everyone asking if you passed when you actually failed and gave the examiner whiplash due to heavy breaking and a brutal emergency stop... awful. Mental note made.

It was a week and a day later when the call came, and it was the longest lapse of time ever in my life. The phone rang and it was John, the producer. My nervous brain struggled to recall any of the conversation apart from the bit where he said "...and we'd like to offer you the part of Trisha..."

My brain then exploded, my face lit up and I thankfully managed to remember how to string a sentence together. Mum was next to me punching the air silently, and I managed a "Wow! Thank you so much! I'd like to formally accept!" in response. I could hear John's smile down the phone as he then said, "And extra congratulations are in order as you're the first person we've cast in the entire series." A huge feather in my cap.

My contract was promptly sent to me along with scripts, and I was asked to come in again to the BBC to assist with the casting process. That's right, ME - on the other side of the audition process. I didn't quite realise at the time just what a privilege that was, but I knew it was very, very cool. To be sitting in that room with the director, casting director, camera assistant and producer, as one after another each girl was brought in to audition with me. Seeing our chemistry on camera as we acted out our 'best of friends but still rivals' scenes, it was all so insightful! More so just to hear what they said about each girl after she left. Each one entered full of hope, nerves, cockiness or desperation, knowing their life or immediate future hinged on this performance, having stressed over it all night and all the way here. All the execs seemed genuinely blasé, nonchalantly commenting, "She was quite good," when each one left. They were more preoccupied with where they were ordering lunch from and were highly fatigued, just wanting to get the damn thing cast so that they could go home. It may not be the same for every casting, but I found it fascinating being on the other side!

That night when I rammed on a rush hour tram home with my scripts under my arm, the young lad whose armpit I was squished into was gazing in awe at my scripts. I had failed to notice at first that they'd printed 'STRICTLY PRIVATE AND CONFIDENTIAL – SHOOTING SCRIPT-Episode 1- Phil McIntyre TV Productions' at the top. I'd placed them not so subtly facing outwards in my clear plastic, zip-lock folder for all the world to see, my pink highlighter pen glowing in the seated tram commuters faces as it lit up all my lines. I glanced down to check he wasn't staring down my top, then remembered I don't dress that way. His eyes were busy checking out my scripts and I was more than happy for him to do so. It took me all my willpower not to blurt out, "So cool, isn't it?! Bet you've never seen a real-life TV script before?! Neither had I till I got this part!" But wisely I stayed silent and let him maybe think I was some kind of celebrity, or try to work out where he might have seen me before. Maybe one day I would actually get asked, "Hey! Aren't you that girl from that thing?" or be recognised in public! Although if and when that does happen, I probably won't be rammed on a tram at rush hour.

Before long I'd received all six scripts for each episode, each one as fat as the last. Going through and highlighting my lines in pink was a joy, and the further I read the more it resonated with me: The ice rink humour, the truth behind it all, the northern tone and my character herself was literally me! I was basically playing myself but that wasn't the best bit...

The series builds up following myself and rival Shannon to the British championships in the final episode and I WIN it. That's right. I'm going to win the British championships on national TV with more people watching than there ever were at the actual British, and hopefully the school bullies, Daniel and Mrs Wiles too. All tuning in to see me win the title I was so unfairly denied. This would be the sweetest feeling ever and the perfect revenge!

Spoiler alert: as I turned the final pages of the final episode, there was a true to life twist; I'd end up getting disqualified as a rival coach doped me with an illegal painkiller, after a crazy Irish girl took me out in the warm-up and I had to perform with a heavily bandaged, bleeding leg. This was brilliant! Who wrote this? Give them a medal! A great twist and bittersweet ending, setting it up perfectly for a second series. This was just the beginning. This was like my skating life played out on TV, with the most true-to-life scenes, such as me watching painfully as the wrong girl gets unjustly crowned as champion, and my coach comforts me saying "Everyone knows who the real winner was today, Trisha," while she comfortingly rubs my shoulder saying, "There's always next year..." Cut to the crazy caretaker and fellow skaters rushing to give me a papier-mâché trophy, still soggy with glue, to make me feel better... Genius!

Chapter 14 – A Whole New World

There was a lot to look forward to before we even began filming, such as the official read-through. This is where we would sit round a table with all the cast members at BBC HQ and read through the entire series together, while enjoying a posh lunch spread catered for by Marks and Spencer's. Proper fancy actor's food! I nailed all the prawn sandwiches while rubbing shoulders with my new colleagues, who'd all been on big shows such as Coronation Street or Midsomer Murders. And then (somewhat miraculously), there's little old me, who'd never set foot in drama school and the only accent I'd learned at school was fake praying in tongues using vegetable names. Plus, I didn't even have an agent or manager. I was a complete unknown. Unless you'd caught the documentary about me and maybe remembered a home-schooled ice skater from Manchester who swallows her toothpaste, and ultimately dumped all her partners?

Then we had the styling and makeovers, where the head of make-up took me to the most expensive salon in Manchester for a cut and colour to reflect my character.

"She's meant to be very dowdy so let's go a mousier brown, some bad highlights and an 'unkept wallflower' kind of look," she declared. Hmm, Not the glamorous TV makeover I was expecting!

"Oh, and can you stop plucking your eyebrows from now until we've wrapped filming? We need them bushy and ungroomed looking."

Are you kidding me? Ok, suck it up, Sophie. At least they're not asking you to shave your head for the role, it could be worse. Besides, you're an actress now! Honestly, I would have probably let them do anything to me, even if it did mean scalping me. It worked for Natalie Portman after all.

I was slightly perturbed when they sent me home with damp hair, as head makeup artist Debbie said my character definitely wouldn't require a blow dry, and she needed to get some Polaroids of my finished 'look', to be recreated in the make-up trailer each morning. Thankfully I was only heading to Primark after this, so I scrunched it up into a messy bun.

I was living for episode 6, though, where I'd get the full hair and make-up treatment (and maybe a spray tan) for the competition scenes!

Then there was the fun day with Head of Wardrobe and Costume Design, Darren, and his assistant Michelle, which was set to be the shopping spree of all shopping sprees! Darren was the most beautiful gay man with an effortless eye for style. I loved the heart-warming dynamic between him and his assistant, who was the complete ungroomed opposite of him; with her greasy hair, no makeup and scoffing a sausage roll whenever we'd pass a Greggs. We didn't have time to eat, and Darren didn't anyway. He was steeped in the fashion world darling, and ran on coffee and cigarettes, while Michelle dusted pastry flakes off her chest. Darren did warn me we wouldn't be stopping for lunch, and I was more than happy to power through as, let's face it, this was the first time I was being taken on a massive shopping spree with a stylist and assistant – all paid for by the BBC – to get all the necessary clothes for my character. I could happily go without a Subway for lunch.

It dawned on me pretty quickly that this wasn't going to be the showbizzy shopping spree I'd hoped... After hitting Primark and vintage shops to seek out the dowdiest, ugliest looking knitwear, mittens and leg warmers, we moved onto Manchester's biggest Asda supermarket for mumsy looking leggings, itchy jumpers and all-round homeless chic. A shopping spree at George at Asda wasn't really on my dream list and I realised I'd drawn the short straw after speaking with my onscreen bestie, who was flying high from her character's shopping day.

"Oh my God Soph, it was amazing! We literally bought the whole Nike store, Miss Sixty jeans, Ted Baker, all the named brands and I got a £280 hairdo and full head of highlights! Where did they take you?" she asked excitedly.

"George at Asda. And a mothball smelling vintage shop," I replied disappointedly.

We were told we could keep whatever we wanted from our character's wardrobe once we'd finished filming too, but obviously I wouldn't be taking them up on this kind offer. I sucked it up as at least I got the part, and I would be able to buy my own Miss Sixty jeans once I got my first TV actress paycheck, which was more money than I'd ever seen at age 15 I remembered saving up my farm wages for months to drop £65 on the new Miss Sixty's with the zip at the back, even though they didn't fit me properly. I could get back to being my usual glam self once I was out of character.

I was reminded how lucky I still was when we got to the Asda checkout, and the checkout lady was buzzing for us at the amount of shit we were buying.

"Wow! Look at all this! Is it someone's birthday? Are you going on holiday?" she asked, smiling at us all. We must have looked like some kind of dysfunctional family: Darren with his immaculate preppy style and glowing tan, Michelle looking like she'd had a tough paper round, and me, stood there beaming, knowing the real answer to her question. But I was following Darren's lead when I notice he just smiled, then subtly ignored her. Probably wise, as if he'd have said, "We're shopping for the cast of a new TV show that's starting filming in a couple of weeks," it would've opened a Pandora's box of questions that she'd start firing at us. It wasn't something you hear every day. Especially not in this store. More like "We need to get rid of this dirty cash!" That would have been a much more fitting answer.

After several sleepless nights fuelled by excitement, vivid dreams, new job nerves, memorising lines and the apprehension of stepping into the complete unknown (and not wanting to screw this up), the day came for me to pack up my stuff and move to the Windsor Hotel in Whitley Bay, where I'd be living for the next eight weeks of filming. It was a long way from home and my first time away from home that lasted longer than two weeks, after Canada's training trip didn't work out. I felt so ready and couldn't wait for my first day on set. I had arrived by train after travelling up the East Coast and they had sent a driver to collect me from the station. I thought they'd got the wrong person when this brand new, shiny, blacked-out Mercedes van pulled up. The electric door slid open revealing a plush leather interior, LED lights, little bottles of water and a smartly dressed driver.

"Miss Portland?" he asked. I took a retardedly long time to reply as my immediate reaction was, "Nope. Wrong person!" But then I remembered I'd chosen 'Portland' as my stage surname after the actor's union, Equity, required me to change it. I'd have to get used to answering to this, just like I quickly got used to answering to my character's name instead. It's a hard thing when someone tells you to pick a stage name. Picking your own name isn't usually something anyone has to do because, hopefully, your parents have done it for you. But I was walking down Portland Street in Manchester and thought "Sophie Portland... Yes. That'll do!" I thought it sounded like a posh British actress name.

As I was transported to the hotel and my soon-to-be new home for the next few months, I gazed through the tinted windows as we zipped along the streets of the run-down North East seaside town. In its heyday it was clearly a once-sought-after seaside destination in the Victorian era. With its once-beautiful ornate architecture and the now-peeling paint work on bandstands and cornices, it resembled a smaller, less-loved Blackpool that time forgot. We passed grotty B&B after grotty B&B, and I did start to worry where they were actually putting me up. Thankfully we arrived at a big, modern, newly renovated hotel that stuck out like a sore thumb. This would do nicely! I was even more pleasantly surprised when I got to my room and it seemed to be upgraded. It was a huge double room at the end of the corridor, so nice and quiet and secluded, with an enormous sunken bathroom complete with marble steps down to it, and more than enough space to line up my many products. I could have lived in the bathroom alone! I knew I was going to be more than happy here as I unpacked, settled down and ordered room service while learning my lines ready for my first day on set.

While devouring my tuna salad on my bed, surrounded by scripts, feeling like the biggest movie star ever, I was disturbed by a rustle at the door. A sheet of paper suddenly shot under it, sliding out onto the floor. It was my call sheet for tomorrow with everyone's call times on it, including what time I was due in hair and makeup, wardrobe and on set.

Shooting was 7 till 7 most days and my call time was often 5:15. As if by magic, I then got a phone call from Gabby, who was going to be my chaperone/ assistant. She'd ensure the car was there to pick me up and take me to the set each morning, where she'd meet me, get me settled in for hair and make-up, while walkie talkie-ing through to catering to get me beans on toast on brown to eat while I sat there. I'd like to say I got transformed in that make-up chair but in reality, my character required the least effort and preening.

They scraped my hair into a bun, put nothing but Carmex on my lips, a tiny bit of brown mascara on my top lashes and fluffed up my eyebrows, I'd barely finished my beans by the time they'd finished with me. I adored sitting there, though, and chatting to the make-up girls, as I looked back at myself in the lightbulb-framed mirror, likely wishing I too got to wear false eyelashes and make-up like everyone else, but still feeling like a star. I was a star: having the blacked-out Mercedes van pick me up every morning, and Gabby literally standing there just to hold my coat or put it round me as soon as they yelled "cut." I was appreciating and loving every moment of the experience, still pinching myself that I was even there! I couldn't understand why all the other actors were kicking off about the work conditions and complaining about how cold and grotty it was. Come on, guys! It's a flippin' ice rink! And yes, I admit it was pretty bad when one of the sound guys got rushed to hospital after ingesting rat poison from picking cables off the dirty floor – but still, an ice rink was my natural habitat.

The lady who played my mum wasn't particularly easy to warm to. She was a classically trained actor with some impressive credits and put herself a cut above everyone else. She even demanded her own private dressing room so she didn't hang with the rest of us in the actors' green room, and only really conversed with me while we were on set and the script told her to. Zoe (my onscreen rival and best friend), on the other hand, got on like a house on fire with her onscreen mum Caroline, who was super cool! She was a huge support to both me and Zoe, encouraging us, believing in us and always checking we were okay, both on and off set, while my own TV mum refused to laugh at my jokes. I didn't care! Everyone else did, and I was just happy to be there.

It was a real bubble of an environment, though, and I soon began picking up on atmospheres, tensions or flirtations amongst cast and crew as the dynamics developed. Ultimately, we were all overworked and under pressure. Many of us were away from family, friends or loved ones for long periods of time and only seeing or conversing with the people surrounding us on set. Or for some, it was the hotel bar.

A couple of things that really stood out in my memory at this time was walking into the green room as things were getting heated between three of the biggest named actors. One was arguing that making it onto a long-running, well-known sitcom as a recurring character should definitely not be seen as the pinnacle of any acting career. And to be in theatre in London's West End was far more 'pure' and admired amongst actors. The other actor (who actually was in a well-known, well-loved sitcom for many years) was fiercely defending this. Obviously. I don't think they noticed me walk in so I sat myself down in the corner, nonchalantly melting my Bounty bar by the rotating fan heater. While others chipped in, I couldn't help but think what a bunch of divas! I'd quite happily take a long running role on Coronation Street for three grand a week, thank you very much.

Fellow skater-turned actress Zoe shared that huge common ground with me, but that's where our similarities ended. She too took it all with a pinch of salt and was so much like her character I struggled to differentiate when she was acting or just talking about her weekend plans. Or "Sunday plans," I should say, as we only got that one day off.

"Aye, I canny wait to go clubbing with me Mam on Saturday and get absolutely rat-arsed shitfaced on blue Wicked's and not even care if I'm flashing me knickers!" she squealed, with an almost inaudible strong Geordie accent. She was hilarious! She'd come out with things and I'd think she was running lines, as I desperately fumbled through my script to remind myself what my line was after her, but most of the time she was just being Zoe in real life. The fact that she'd go underage clubbing with her mum at the weekends, and genuinely did plan on spending her TV wages on a boob job as soon as she was 18, made me realise the casting on this show was spot on. She really did wear caked-on silver eye shadow from her lid to her brows in real life, and I'd crease up more than that eye shadow while overhearing her conversations with her mum:

"Yeah, so me mate Gemma's coming over about 1pm on Saturday before we head out to the toon!" Zoe said, excitedly.

"Good idea, so you'll start getting ready from 1pm?" her mum asked.

"NO! We start pre drinking at 1pm Mam, then getting ready from 5. Christ- we're not that fucking ugly!!"

I would die! We couldn't be more different. Although I had a lot more scenes and lines than she did, I really enjoyed our scenes together when we did have them. But no, I never took her up on her offer to join them on their boozy nights out where the bouncers didn't ask for ID!

Chapter 15 – Things Are Not What They Seem

There was a seedy side to the 'filming on location' world.
Much like the world of a cruise ship show skater, I imagine.

Late one night, after my room service dinner and
learning lines, I heard one of the guys from set design,
Marcus (who's room neighboured mine), open his door to a
late-night visitor. I'd often hear him yawning or his nightly
phone calls to his long-term girlfriend back home as they
spoke about their days at work and upcoming holiday plans.
The walls were thin and it sounded like he had a girl in his
room. Surely not? Maybe the knock on his door was room
service and he was now on the phone to his girlfriend and
put her on loudspeaker. I switched my lights off and told
myself to stop being so nosey and go to sleep. But I couldn't
help thinking I knew that girl's voice... It was Lara, one of
the runners! Then the sounds of cans of beer opening,
followed by small talk and then it started...I really didn't want
to hear what I was hearing, and wished I could fill my ears
up with cement. I was horrified. Disgusted in fact, that he
could cheat on his girlfriend so easily and that Lara was
happy to play a part in this, knowing full well of his situation,
often asking about his post-filming holiday plans in the
catering truck. I lay there in disbelief, wishing I could block
it all out. And equally wishing I could hammer on his door
while screaming, "YOU CHEATING PIG!" and maybe writing
LOVE RAT on his door in a Sharpie pen. Or maybe I'd start
screaming in the background of his next phone call to his
girlfriend that she should dump him ASAP. I guess it didn't
go on for that long, but it felt like a slow eternity. I jumped
out of bed when I heard her leaving and sure enough, it was
her. I watched their final kiss through the peephole. What
vile, moral-less humans!

Looking back and still to this day, that sort of thing probably happens all the time within these industries, but it was a shock to my system. I had never been exposed to it before and always assumed that most people were good. I still do. Shortly after she left, Marcus sickeningly rang his girlfriend telling her how much he missed her and echoed back, "What have I been up to? Oh, not much babe, was on set late tonight so just got back." It made my skin crawl and blood boil. As much as I wanted to expose them both, and save Marcus's girl from jetting off to a tropical island with such a lying, disgusting prick, I resorted to making Lara highly uncomfortable in the make-up truck. I'd ask if she'd had a late night and watched her squirm as she desperately tried to deliver a feasible answer, seriously making her question if I did indeed know the truth. As for Marcus, I contemplated subtly moving small props on set so he'd get in trouble for continuity issues, but settled for saying a quick prayer each day that his willy would fall off instead.

Cheating crewmembers and primadonna actors aside, my time in run-down Whitley Bay being a proper little TV actress, were some of the happiest days of my life. There was always something funny, exciting, different or challenging happening, even if it was just me making it fun in my own head. Every day it came down to the fact that I was simply so happy to be there, doing something I loved without the worry of dance partners, judges or the next competition looming.

"Hey Sophie, can you do a banana into shot, please!" commanded the first AD, which required me to skate into shot in a curve. I looked confused.

"You've done a banana before, right?"

"I've never done any type of fruit to be honest," I replied. There was always a laugh to be had and a smile to be raised in my opinion, as while we were all working extremely hard, it was so important to dilute the stress and tensions with some humour. We were making a comedy after all!!

In one of the early scenes, there was a girl who didn't have any lines, but her character was attacked by a hawk that was nesting in the rink's rafters. I watched as she had to have a chunk of raw dead rabbit attached to her hood, causing this enormous bird of prey to swoop in on cue, sending her crashing to the ground, face down. Not only that, she was the most unfortunate looking, shy girl. When she was waiting in the green room, I couldn't help but notice she was painfully ugly and even appeared to have an abnormal amount of shadowy facial hair for a girl so young (and a girl in general). I thanked my lucky stars my role didn't require me to have rabbit meat pinned to me, have a bird of prey attack me or be cursed with a lifetime of upper lip waxes. I often texted mum while waiting for my scenes, as I'd always liked to tell her what interesting and random things were happening on set. And that day, it mostly involved feeling terribly sorry for this poor, hairy girl in the glittery pink skating dress. Imagine my confusion when one of the runners came in calling, "Roger! We're ready for you now," and said hairy girl jumps up. It was a man! A stuntman in fact. I watched as he sauntered past me in his Lycra dress, readjusting his balls. I'd never been so relieved to see a man in skating tights before, as it suddenly all made sense. I was VERY glad I didn't put my foot in it by saying something like I usually would, and it also reminded me that nothing or no one are what they seem in this TV world...

I had to wear my own fair share of ugly or weird costumes throughout the episodes. Like a diamond-studded eye patch and cape when I performed to Gabrielle, which turned out to be unbelievably hard, throwing off my balance and constantly causing me to veer to the left.

Or the skating dress of nightmares, which Darren from wardrobe kindly had made for me when he asked me to describe my "dress from hell." This was for the episode where all the other skaters had fancy competition dresses and I couldn't afford one, so had to step out in a badly made peach-and-white coloured monstrosity with a tutu skirt, huge puffed sleeves, a massive bow at the back and flesh body stocking, which wrinkled and was a million miles away from my actual skin tone. Darren nailed it; I'll give him that! But I most definitely would not be keeping this horrific creation once filming wrapped. One of the extras, however (a real life super-cute skater gran), kept telling me how beautiful my dress was whenever they'd shout "cut." She genuinely loved it. I melted a bit inside, seeing how, from her era, puffed sleeves and peach satin really was the thing.

Another cool experience was doing my own stunts! Thankfully, no hawk or animal meat were required. This was for the scene at the British Championships where a crazy girl from Belfast took me out in the warm-up, impaling her blade in my leg and putting my ability to compete in serious doubt. Cue: little old me, throwing myself onto an out of shot crash pad repeatedly, followed by fake blood and giving myself the worst whiplash of my life – all before we broke for lunch. Like everything, I gave it maximum effort (and probably a little too much) in order to get a great shot, and I relished the thought that I was now an 'actress who does her own stunts' and doesn't have facial hair! My onscreen mum was appalled I'd not demanded a stunt double and couldn't understand it. But I was quite happy for them not to call Roger back and I'd have a go myself. She also clearly didn't know I was used to being swung around by my thighs by a guy who threatened to drop me, so voluntarily throwing myself on a crash pad for a whole camera crew and getting paid well for it was an absolute pleasure.

Continuing with the 'nothing or no one are what they seem' theme, for the British Championship scenes, rather than hiring thousands of extras, they hired an inflatable crowd. Something that had been done in many big Hollywood movies and, at the time, the hit Wimbledon movie. Real people would be interspersed with the inflatable ones, and it really was hard to tell at times who was real and who wasn't. I freaked out momentarily when a girl in the crowd in front of me punched the guy next to her in his head. Hard, leaving him leaning motionless on his side, presumed dead. Thankfully I soon realised he wasn't real, and she was just cold and bored. There was so much to get done and we were running dangerously behind schedule. It was many characters' final day on set, and many of their partners were turning up in the green room as they'd wait for them to wrap, while having a nosy to figure out where their other half had been living and working over these past hectic weeks. I chat to anyone and I'd often feel sorry for the bored looking wives or boyfriends, who'd come and watch their other halves doing their thing in a world no doubt completely different from their own. Most of the time they must have been so confused. (As you would be if you'd rocked up at an ice rink with an inflatable crowd, rat traps and me, with a leg covered in fake blood.) Or they might be losing the will to live, as they watched them do take after take of the same thing. I took it upon myself to strike up conversation with one of the guys who'd been there for hours, watching his wife from the green room window, repeatedly having to mime clap, with a large group of extras for an orchestrated shot. He must have been so baffled!

"It's weird, isn't it?!" I quipped. "They do this a lot in telly... They're getting them to mime the applause and then they'll dub it at a later date. It looks like that's what they're doing now... And all those people not clapping are inflatable! Just like in big movies!" I added, excitedly.

"That's fascinating!" he smiled calmly, and preceded to ask me about my time here, if I'd enjoyed the experience and if I had any other jobs lined up. He was such a lovely man, super chilled and I bet so looking forward to getting his wife back. After telling him about more of my favourite learning experiences on a proper TV set, and how famous some of the other cast members were, I was interrupted by one of the runners calling me to set. They were ready for me!

"Oh! That's me! Well, it was lovely to meet you. What was your name again sorry?" (I was terrible with names and something I still have to work on). He laughed.

"Well, it was lovely to meet you too, Sophie. I'm Andy. Good luck with everything!" he called, as I left him in the warm glow of the green room fan heater. Imagine the whole new levels of mortified I felt when a matter of days later, when the popular morning show, "This Morning," was on TV and who was sat on the sofa as star guest but Andy! The bored but friendly guy from the green room. He only happened to be the guy famous for playing Gollum in Lord of the Rings and King Kong in the new King Kong movie. My jaw dropped and my head exploded as it flashed back to our conversation where I took pity on him, explaining to him what was going on on-set, assuming he had no knowledge or experience of anything happening around him. I must have come across as the most condescending, uneducated idiot by not knowing what a huge, iconic movie star he was. He would have been quite within his rights to drop the "Do you know who I am?" line, and I deserved it. I died 1000 deaths and still do. Even more so when I Googled him and his Wikipedia said he was one of the highest grossing actors of all time, and had been critically acclaimed for his work. There I was explaining to him about mime clapping and dubbing. Kill me now! I rang my mum immediately to share my embarrassment and all she kept saying was what a nice man he must have been to listen to me waffle on and not put me in my place...which would have deservedly been the biggest hole ever that I had rapidly dug for myself. We live and learn. Well, I'd love to say I do, but as you read on, you'll see I am a regular at putting my foot in it, and the most painfully cringeworthy moments will have made it into this book.

Chapter 16 – Down But Not Out

When the final day of filming rolled round, it suddenly dawned on me that this magical TV filming world and way of life was coming to an end. The people I'd grown so close with I most likely would never see again, unless we happened to work on the same production together in future. I wouldn't be living in a posh hotel, learning lines every night, getting picked up each morning by my driver, working the longest days but thriving on the excitement and adrenaline of it all. Everything from here on in was going to feel like the biggest anti-climax. I'd had a taste of this world now, and I knew it was for me, although I was only basing that off one great job. I also realised how special it was to be in the last scene of the last day filming, when the director yelled "Cut!" for the final time and "That's a wrap!" We all cheered, hugged, high fived and many of us got a little teary-eyed. By the time we'd released our embraces, the crew had already sprung into action, de-rigging everything. Articulated lorries rolled into the car park to load the enormous lights, blackouts, scaffolding and other pieces of set. It was amazingly slick but also sad how quickly everything was disappearing around us. I felt extra proud that day, though, as mum had driven up and was on-set for my final hours of being 'Trisha'. I'd only seen her once throughout the entire 10 weeks filming. Partly because I only had one day off, and it was a trek to go from South Shields to Manchester and back again in a day, but mainly because I didn't want to come home. I was living the dream so hard! I didn't want to step out of my actress life even for a day. She knew I was happy and could more than look after myself, when she saw the size of my marble bathroom and the huge fruit bowl I'd got for myself to sit on my dressing table, tumbling with fresh grapes and a bowl of fancy Marks and Spencer's cashew nuts beside it. Everyone was so excited to meet her. They all said how they couldn't get over how happy I was ALL THE TIME. While everyone else was moaning, there I was, always smiling.

"How is she so happy all the time?" they joked. Mum overflowed with pride as they went on to say what a joy I was to have on set, and they'd work with me again in a heartbeat. This was lovely to hear, but I never believed I was any more special than the next person. I was just a girl living an unexpected dream.

Naturally, the end of shoot conversations soon turned to what jobs other people were going on to (or lack of). The bigger named actors with the bigger influence agents were already booked for other roles on shows filming straight after this. Seeing how hard it was going to be for mere mortals like me and Zoe going back to mundane real life, they all assured us the show would almost certainly be coming back for a second and third series. That's what usually happens with shows like this, and the storyline had been left wide open for the follow-up series. After all, the evil coach, who purposefully doped me and got me disqualified in the final episode, needed to get her comeuppance in series two. The blossoming character romances needed to develop, and we would all want to know if Zoe's character really did get her much talked about boob job and new car. They seemed pretty certain this would go ahead, so at least we had that to look forward to.

Because we'd fallen behind schedule, there was some scenes still left to film, and lucky for me, I was in them and they were filming at BBC in Manchester. I was becoming a regular at that place! Not so lucky for me though, I came down with tonsillitis a matter of days before filming. I'd never had it before and, without realising it, had gotten a little run down; but under no circumstances could I afford to miss this day. The whole crew, premises and fellow actors had all been booked for this and most of the missing scenes were mine! I did not have time to be ill, but I barely had a voice. When I swallowed it was like choking on razor blades. I had some big scenes ahead of me that required me to cry and have a screaming argument with my on-screen mum. A tall order for any actress at the best of times. Mum came along with me as human paracetamol dispenser and mime translator. It was wonderful to see some of my former colleagues, albeit a much more scaled down cast and crew. Walking back into the BBC made me realise how much I'd achieved in such a short space of time, when now my pass said 'Artist' instead of 'Visitor'. I'd be ill and dying tomorrow. Today- I had work to do.

The morning's scenes didn't go too badly, as director Sarah assured me we could dub my lines at a later date when I was feeling better. Cool! I bet even Andy Serkis would agree. My biggest and most emotional scene was the last of the day, so when we broke for lunch at 12, I knew I still had to try to remain on voice rest. It was almost impossible for someone like me, as I wanted to catch up and gossip with everyone. We all had to walk around the block to a nearby hotel that they had booked to provide our lunch. I'll never forget that meal as it was the driest salmon I've ever had in my life, and I resorted to eating a bowl of ice cream instead. One of the only perks to having tonsillitis! Or so I thought. It turned out to actually work in my favour, as when that emotionally charged final scene came, I sounded like I'd been crying hysterically for days! It worked perfectly, despite me feeling like I might die and permanently damage my voice box. I was so happy with how it turned out and more importantly, so was producer John.

As you might have guessed, I did have to re-record some of my lines but even this turned out to be a joy as they whisked me to London to record in a tiny, historic London studio nestled in Soho. I was beyond excited. When I was put in that fancy sound booth, my immediate response to the sound guy asking for a mic check was, "Wow, all the walls are padded! Even if I fall over, it's okay! This is great!" – like I was some kind of basket case.

I was there less than an hour, so I had the rest of the day to explore London, feeling like a star and dying to tell someone I was here for 'ADR' ('Additional dialog recording' to you and I). I didn't realise at the time but as that day was out of contract, they paid me an additional fee, resulting in me getting paid the most money I'd ever earned in a day (or 45 minutes), eclipsing that of even my parents' best earning day in their careers. It might only be a one-off so I was saving every penny but technically, I could go out and buy seven and a half pairs of Nike shox! Aged 16, my life had peaked.

In theory, there should have been many more exciting days to come as all the promo kicked in for the six episodes of 'Thin Ice': radio interviews, TV interviews, magazine promo shoots, photoshoots for adverts, and general buzz created in the run- up to the show airing. But there was a new skating show about to drop. And this one had definitely not been done before...

Celebrities on Ice was set to be the next big show another giant television network was ploughing all their money into, with Olympic legends Torvill and Dean fronting it. The current Winter Olympics were also happening and, all of a sudden, ice skating was hot property. To coincide with the timing of both these other huge skating events, it was decided by the powers that be that they would rush to get our ice-themed comedy out at the same time. This meant hardly any time for promo and advertising build-up, a rushed edit, a rubbish time slot and an all-round rough deal. Obviously, we all told everyone we could think of to watch it. Mum even got all the nuns at the convent to watch it as they'd known her since she was four and me since I was a bump. I probably should have warned everyone that episode two contained a lot of lewd jokes and S&M equipment, as a shed load of the stuff was discovered in the ice rink storeroom and was a funny, risqué part of the storyline. I did feel like I'd sinned massively at the thought of all these cute, old nuns sat around with their cups of tea, having to endure these very rude but equally hilarious scenes as they waited for me to skate on. But let's hope it was a refreshing change for them after their usual routine of evening prayer.

I appreciated any ratings it could get, as good ratings meant series two and three would be firmly in the pipeline. I'd religiously go into any newsagents every week when all the new TV guides would come out, and buy every copy of Heat magazine, TV Times or newspapers, if it had my picture in it or even quoted my name. 'Starring Sophie Portland' and whoever else's name they chose to quote that week. Much to my superfan Nana's delight, I was in all the local papers with nice little interviews, and photographers were sent round to snap pictures of me grinning with my skates to accompany the print. Much to my own delight (and sweet taste of revenge), I knew Mrs Wiles and the bitchy girls would be watching. Purely out of curiosity if nothing else. Mrs Wiles already knew about my previous achievements as my mum generously sent her the newspaper article of when I won the Scottish Championships, and attached my last school report where she'd written "Sophie lacks drive and determination..." I still enjoy a sweet tasting smile whenever I think of this. It felt SO good!

Tuesday nights became the biggest night of the week for those six weeks, and our phones would all go crazy after every episode. There wasn't social media back then (I know, weird right?). But there were those dodgy Internet chat rooms or message boards full of keyboard warriors. I chose not to read them, but I was told the only people slating it were the self-confessed ice-skating purists, completely horrified at how their perfect sport had been portrayed. They clearly didn't like it that, killer Hawks and S&M equipment aside, it was very true to life and the bizarre, exciting, backstabbing, magical and intense skating underworld had been exposed. It also was quite possibly Daniel posting under multiple different accounts, eaten up with jealousy that his ex-skating partner was on the TV and he was now obese and working for Vodafone. Karma is a beautiful thing!

I'd dared to let myself dream that this could be the start of something big for me, or at least get another couple of series out of it. But despite all our efforts, newspaper articles and mother superiors watching, the ratings didn't make the cut. This was gutting for all of us: cast, crew, writers and especially the lighting guy who ingested rat poison for this! It was a bitter pill indeed.

After this whirlwind six months, I decided the actor's life was for me. I'd been well and truly bitten by the acting bug but clueless as to where to go from here. I needed some guidance and that's where Zoe's onscreen mum Caroline stepped in. Although we didn't have many scenes together, she had been an on-set mum to us all, always there for us to help with lines, to offer words of encouragement or just to have a laugh about my inability to drag on those fake cigarettes for a certain scene. We met for lunch in Manchester one rainy afternoon after the show had aired and debriefed it all. She was singing my praises and injected some much-needed confidence in me with her kind words of support. I realised at that moment she believed in me far more than I believed in myself. First things first, I needed an agent, followed by some decent headshots. She hooked me up with both! Putting me in touch with one of her old agents and the guy who did her pictures. Within a week, I was walking into one of Manchester's biggest skyscrapers for a chat or should I say subtle begging of a "please sign me" style meeting with a potential agent. It all felt like a good omen, as it just so happened to be in the very building my grandad Poppa once worked in, and they signed me on the spot. I now could legitimately say, "You'll have to speak to my agent," and enjoyed thinking of potential scenarios in my head when I could use this line. Although I don't think I ever have, apart from when a creepy traffic warden asked for my number and resorted to giving me his instead, by slapping it on my windscreen in an official parking penalty notice packet, for me to find on my return. He signed it 'Tom, the naughty Traffic Warden'. I couldn't help but fear for his lifetime of singleness if this is how he tried to pick up girls.

Chapter 17 – A Jobbing Actress

Newly signed to agency books and with headshots snapped, I was ready to hit the auditioning circuit. It didn't take me long to realise that auditions could be very few and far between, especially as back then, there weren't a lot of roles for young girls that didn't require me to be an utter slag. As many jobbing actors do, it was time for me to get a part-time job to work in between my hopefully frequent roles.

I was over 16 now which meant I could finally get paid minimum wage, a whole £5 an hour, and work in an actual shop! I'd had three wonderful years working weekends on the farm, but now I was on to pastures new and getting paid into my bank account, not in a little brown envelope. It had always been a little goal of mine to work at the once fancy but slightly outdated mini department store in Altrincham, Rackhams. I liked the idea of working in the glossy cosmetics and fragrance department, wearing court shoes instead of wellies, and coming home smelling of the latest Calvin Klein instead of horse manure.

I waltzed in with my short but punchy CV and had an interview with the ultra-gorgeous cosmetics floor manager. Although my only experience was in competitive ice dancing, feeding rabbits and livestock, being on TV and blowing vast amounts of Canadian dollars in a short space of time, she offered me a job there and then, and I started that weekend.

I worked in the fragrance department. Also known as 'the back wall'. I soon realised it was mind numbingly boring and severely unstimulating for me. People clearly never walked that far back in the store. It was dead and I'd spend most of my time helping old ladies to buy fragranced soaps that smelled like cheap air fresheners, or talcum powder. I was amazed the store managed to stay open, judging by the low footfall it had. But still, it had a Chanel counter so it mustn't have been doing too bad, unless Lucinda on that Chanel counter in the window was scaring everyone off. She was hellish fierce and would keep a padlock on her samples drawer. Probably wise, as people would kill their granny for a free mini mascara.

As I'd drift up the escalator to the staff room on my break, I'd gaze at the silver grooves of the steps folding away from me, mesmerising me in my bored state, making me question how my life had gone from a TV set to this... A grotty staff canteen with a mouldy microwave, and the only thing to muse over was the guy from menswear, who would cut his Mars bar into seven pieces, and only allow himself a cube a day on his lunch breaks. I'd watch in amazement as he'd make that Mars bar last all week.

It wasn't where I wanted to be, but I kept reassuring myself it was a stopgap and I'd be outta here in a flash, as soon as I booked my next big acting role. I still gave it my all as that was my default behaviour, and soon became staff member of the month, receiving 100% in two consecutive mystery shops. I was also in the top five for getting customers to sign up to a store card, which I now realise was the devil's work, but they used to let me go home 15 minutes early for every one I sold, which meant I didn't have to cash up. I can still to this day recite the phonetic alphabet because of it.

It would appear to me, though, that even in the most boring of professions, it wasn't without scandal...

I was shocked when the women's wear manager was suddenly sacked for shoplifting as she'd purchased a Ralph Lauren T-shirt for her dad then refunded the money back to her card early the next morning. What a nice daughter. I wonder if he ever wore it after it resulted in her sacking? I also wondered how much other stuff she refunded to herself over the years...

The worst thing, though, was when the fragrance department phone rang, and I was summoned up to the staff training room and was told to bring the first aid box. Maybe they wanted me to pretend I was choking or pretend I'd injured myself so I could finally show off my acting ability with their training role play. I skipped up that old escalator with my little green box, buzzing to be off the shop floor for five minutes. But I wasn't prepared for what I found when I opened the door: my line manager Lucy, completely passed out on the floor. She lay there motionless, with her beautiful hair spread across the carpet and makeup still intact. I thought she'd died! I felt the blood drain from my face and I probably looked worse than she did at that moment.

"Oh my God, is she OK?" I gasped.

"Give me!" Snapped her right-hand woman Kelly, who was kneeling next to her, motioning for me to pass the first aid kit.

"She'll be fine. Now get yourself back on the shop floor and don't breathe a word of this to ANYONE! Understand?"

I nodded. Very much NOT understanding and staggered back down to my fragrance wall, totally speechless.

"Sophie, what's wrong? You look like you've seen a ghost!" one of the girls asked. I couldn't lie, I was so worried for Lucy and visibly shaken. I explained what had just happened and weirdly none of them were surprised. Turns out Lucy had a bad cocaine habit and had obviously taken a bit too much that day, and was literally coked off her face on the training room floor, like it was a standard Tuesday thing! At that point, I'd never seen anyone on drugs before (or so I thought), and assumed the only people that took them were crackheads on the streets. Not the glamorous store managers that granted me my first retail job. I really liked her and looked up to her somewhat, but after this and the phantom refunding manager, I was struggling to maintain the same level of respect for these people in power.

When I wasn't working instore, I was still skating most mornings, but coach Carol was increasingly MIA. She was spending most of her time in London, as she was on the judging panel for that new show we were all talking about, Celebrities on Ice. On one hand, this was incredibly exciting as suddenly everyone was talking about ice skating or wanted to learn. Perfect for me as a trainee coach, as once I qualified, there would be loads of new customers wanting lessons. On the other hand, I myself was without a coach most of the time and she rather selfishly refused to let me train with anyone else in her absence. Saying that I was her skater and nobody else's. But we'd stuck together through thick and thin, so I would continue to do so. It was exciting when I did see her, and she'd confidentially tell me what celebrities they were considering auditioning. It was like getting a weekly inside scoop! The first series was a huge success. More than anyone expected. As optimistic as I was with my almost delusional 'everything's going to work out great' view of life, even I doubted how that show would ever work. Skating is not an easy sport to just take up at any time. Especially if your day job isn't particularly athletic and you're not accustomed to experiencing the centrifugal force felt in spinning lifts, and balancing with blades on your feet while moving at speed. It's all VERY unnatural. When you think about it, the rival show that teaches celebrities to ballroom dance works, because the contestants can already walk. So teaching them to dance should be no issue. But with Celebrities on Ice, they had to learn to skate first, and for the poor male celebrities they also had to learn to lift! While on blades, while moving, while in Lycra, while on live TV. I think I'd even trust Daniel to lift me more than the weatherman from Good Morning Britain. With that said, the show took the country (and soon the world!) by storm. One of Australia's largest TV channels bought the rights for it and were set to do their own version, jumping on the bandwagon as quickly as possible. And who got the call to be the head judge and coach but Carol! I was beyond excited for her and hadn't yet thought what this meant for me: no coach for at least two months, skating round with no purpose and no doubt missing her terribly. Before I even allowed my mind to go to that logical place, she said, "Why don't you come with me? They're putting me up in a three-bed apartment so I can have family come visit me. You could train at the TV studios ice pad and understudy all the female professionals!"

Much like when I randomly got the chance to go to Canada, I didn't have to think twice. All I'd be missing here was boring training sessions at Blackburn, spraying the occasional customer with fragrance and probably picking my coke head manager off the floor. I could use my TV wages to pay for my flight ticket and accommodation was already covered. I'd just need to make sure I had enough money for spends, exploring and watermelon.

I'd just turned 17 and was toying with the idea of spending my money on a pink Nissan Micra or having mums Ford KA resprayed in candy floss pink, but Sydney, Australia, and the thought of being back on some kind of TV set was a much better option. I could pick up my driving lessons when I returned. I was already a natural behind the wheel and had been desperate to drive since I was about nine. Regularly sitting in the driver seat of Dad's car when it was parked in the driveway, visualising turning the wheel and pushing the pedals. (If I could actually reach them). I was that person whose first driving lesson was 10 a.m. on their 17th birthday, and was dangerously excited. Especially after six months of lessons in a driving simulator. To get in a vehicle and actually move somewhere was amazing.

Excitement levels escalated when driving instructor Trevor turned up in a purple Fiesta (so close to pink!) and I spent most of the lesson squealing, "I'M MOVING!"

Despite not stalling once, I probably nearly gave Trevor a heart attack as he did look like he'd just been dug up. It worked out great going to Australia as I was going to change instructors anyway. He was holding me back, clearly wanting to maintain his blood pressure instead of letting me try anything more exciting, like manoeuvres or a high-speed dual carriage way. Joy killer! I brought a bag of cherry tomatoes with me on one lesson to snack on, as I'd read they helped to stimulate your brain. I told him this with such authority, offering him one, but he just looked at me with a pained expression of 'God help me, I've got to spend 2 hours in a car with this girl!'

Whatever, Trevor! I'm breaking up with you for an Australian adventure.

Naturally, the TV network was paying all Carol's expenses, so she was flying business class. She did try to get me upgraded too, saying I was still a minor (true) and a very nervous flyer (far from true), and we really needed to sit together as I was her responsibility.

"We're sorry Mrs Bacon, we can't upgrade her to business class but we can downgrade you to economy?"

"Don't worry – she'll be fine!" Carol answered, without even a second's pause. I can't blame her! At first it wasn't a bad setup... I was towards the front of economy on an aisle seat and she was at the back of business class. We could both lean out into the aisle and wave at one another, mouthing what films we should watch, and she'd send me all her fancy chocolates and gourmet snacks. This was great, until the air hostess pulled the curtain across, dividing the two cabins. Maybe this was out of kindness so we couldn't see all the VIPs living it up in business class, but it felt more like we were diseased peasants, and the mere sight of us was offending the posh people further up the plane.

After a few hours stop and a refuel in Dubai, it felt like the longest flight of my life. The most amount of hours I'd ever spent encased in anything metal. I honestly believed it would never end and this was now my life. Stupidly, I watched that 127 Hours film about the mountain climber who got his arm trapped between a boulder while hiking in a canyon in Utah. He was trapped there for 127 hours, almost dying until he resorted to cutting his own arm off in order to free himself. There I was, sat on a plane feeling trapped and frustrated, watching someone else also feeling trapped and frustrated, while hacking off his own arm. Thankfully, I didn't have to do that, I just had to put up with the cardboard-tasting pretzels. It was a poor film choice purely based on the fact I fancied James Franco.

After that stressful 1 hour and 34 minutes of my life, I thought I'd try to have a sleep. I can't sleep on planes in those uncomfortable upright seats, but thought I would at least try, having been up for probably 20 hours at this point. I definitely drifted off somewhere, probably to a happier place with James Franco. But for how long, I wasn't sure. Cruelly, there was a large screen on the wall in front of us all, displaying the world map and dotted flight path we were taking. It looked like a really shit treasure map with the 'Time to Destination' displayed underneath it. I opened my blurry eyes to see 11:37. Amazing! I'd slept for the rest of the flight! Eleven minutes and 37 seconds to landing. I can sleep on planes after all! I quickly fastened my seat belt and shoved everything under my seat to prepare for landing. As I scanned the cabin, I was confused why no one else looked as ecstatic as me to be getting off this damn plane. I looked back at the screen I'd been trying to ignore and to my horror it now said 11:34... Those were hours and minutes to go, not minutes and seconds! I hung my head and internally wept, vowing to myself that I would not return to Australia until I could afford business class.

Chapter 18 – Adventures Down Under

When we eventually arrived on whatever day it now was, Carol didn't want to get off the plane. I on the other hand, wanted to kiss the ground and felt like Ariel the mermaid when she'd gotten her legs.

Passport control, baggage reclaim and straight into a taxi to take us to our penthouse apartment: let the adventure begin!

They weren't lying when they said 'penthouse'. I'm pretty sure we were at the very top of this ultra-fancy, modern apartment tower, complete with concierge and the shiniest tiles. We appeared to have half of the entire top floor with a wraparound balcony, panoramic floor to ceiling windows and these cool electric shutters on the outside of the glass, controlled by a switch in the kitchen so you could tilt them accordingly. Maybe if it got too sunny or the birds were spying on you perhaps? Honestly, it was an incredible pad! Huge open plan kitchen, dining, living space, with a massive centre island, 12-seater dining table, views out towards the harbour, an enormous plush L-shaped sofa, even bigger TV and the bathrooms? Don't even get me started on the ridiculous size of the walk-in rainfall showers. Oh, and did I mention they'd booked us a weekly cleaner so we didn't even have to lift a finger, and all our marble and glass would remain extra glossy? Australia's biggest TV network clearly had a big budget for this skating show.

My schedule was Carol's schedule as I'd come with her each day to the studio and be skating the whole time she was on the ice. Or I could go and chill in the green room with the celebrities. The nice thing was, I didn't have a clue who any of them were or how famous they were. Some were models, one was famous for being a model that was dating Miss Universe so you can just imagine his level of handsomeness... Others were former pop stars but my favourite one was probably Carl. He'd chat to me for ages and was absolutely hilarious! It wasn't until I switched the TV on one morning and saw him on the sofa of Australia's morning show that I realised he was the equivalent of our Philip Schofield.

I loved learning all the choreography for the professional female skaters so I could step in should any of them get injured. Or sometimes they were just taking too long in the loo. Wherever they were, I was more than happy to leap into action when all the exec producers were watching. I secretly hoped they'd see I was a much better skater than some of their chosen ones: smaller, easy to lift, always smiling and therefore they would immediately replace Miss Universe boyfriend's partner with me. Sadly, this never happened but a girl can dream. Rather irritatingly, I'd caught the eye of another guy. Not a celebrity, but a typical skater boy, currently without a partner and looking for a girl to accompany him on his next Ice show he'd get cast in.

Trent was a show skater, very tall and had retired from competing to live his life dancing on a minute cruise ship ice pad, or playing Jafar in Disney on Ice. He definitely had the large, hooked nose for it and it would constantly be dripping. He was definitely no Miss Universe's boyfriend... As Trent was understudy for the male professionals, he was always there and began to grab me at every opportunity to skate with or practise lifts with. It was fun at first and I got to try some wild lifts I'd never done before. But although he was from down under, he still had all the same obnoxious, condescending, arrogant and spoilt characteristics that the British skater boys had. It was clearly a global trait within their species. He made it very clear that he wanted to go into shows with me and put daily pressure on me that I too should desire the show life. That doing my coaching training was a 'waste of time' and something to only pursue when I physically couldn't perform anymore. I also told him about my potential acting career plans, and he shot them down immediately. I was quickly starting to strongly dislike him and his controlling manner, and the way his massive nose would constantly drip on me when we were in dance hold. Carol was all for this partnership, though, and tried convincing me that going into shows with Trent was a great option, reminding me that's how she met her husband when they were both show skaters. As I explained earlier, it's not something I've ever felt I've wanted to do, especially with the lifestyle that comes with it. I definitely was never going to marry Trent and condemn myself to a lifetime of mopping up his drippy nose. I was trying to get away from him at every opportunity, so would often sneak off to the green room and chat with the celebs or watch Miss Universe's boyfriend doing his warmup stretches.

Another favourite of mine was Cassandra. A former model and visibly paranoid about the 10 years younger version of herself (glamour model Laura) who was also on the show. We'd always have the best girly chats and she'd unknowingly boost my confidence if it was low, like telling me I had such good skin that was "out-of-control good!" A phrase that still makes me smile and can easily be applied to many things; like an awesome new song you hear or a delicious flavour of ice cream you discover.

Despite being blonde and beautiful, she too had her own insecurities. She was extremely upset that her false eyelash was slightly peeling off on the promo shot of her that the channel had plastered over all the giant billboards or bus stops round Sydney. It did make her look a bit cross eyed if I'm honest. She was also convinced that Trent fancied me. I'd tell her I wasn't interested, and he only wants me for my body and leg lines, which, thinking about it, sounds very wrong when you take it out of the skating context.

I was gutted when she was voted off the show first and I wished we could have kept in touch. But that's life when you're working on a TV show. As I found during Thin Ice. You get close to people then before you know it, they're gone.

Time is always of the essence so appreciate it and use it wisely. With that said, it soon dawned on me that my time in Oz would be coming to an end and I'd only seen the inside of an ice rink or our fancy apartment. Once the first male celeb was voted off, his skating partner naturally became the understudy for the rest of the skater girls. I technically wasn't required to be at the studio every morning now and neither was Trent. I couldn't escape him that easy, though. He was constantly texting me to arrange a skate time, and when he rocked up with his parents one morning, because "they'd heard so much about me," I knew we had a problem. And it wasn't the fact I simply couldn't get past his dad's nose. I'm 17, in Sydney for the first time and hadn't even seen a koala or the Opera House yet!

It was time to get out there and explore, whether Trent liked it or not, and even if Carol wasn't okay with letting me out of her sight.

I was due to leave in just under a week, so I compiled a hit list of all the places I wanted to go and things I wanted to see. This would involve water taxis, ferries, a cable car, a camera, spending money and Carol's blood pressure going through the roof. She had two daughters a similar age to me, yet I could tell she didn't give them much freedom. The mere thought of me going sightseeing alone would prompt her to send my mum hourly updates until I was back at the apartment safely. I tried telling her if I could convince a ticket conductor in a Canadian bus station that I was eleven in order to get a cheap ticket, or repeatedly throw myself on the ground for my own stunts when needed, or pray in fake tongues using vegetable names and above all – put up with Daniel – I could more than look after myself around Sydney.

The next morning, I was up early with Carol and we had our tea and toast together as usual. The only difference was today she was heading off to the studio alone and I was unleashing my curious, adventurous, exploring self across the city and its waters. After a rushed and standard mum-style safety talk, off I went. I'd been told to checkout Manly Beach and its trendy surfing and volleyball scene, along with Sydney Harbour Zoo, the Opera House (obvs), Luna Park, the Bondi to Coogee Walk, a stalkerish harbour tour of where the likes of Nicole Kidman and Russell Crowe lived, and the famous Harry's Café de Wheels - even though I don't eat pies.
   I'd compiled this list by talking to Carol's driver on the morning commutes to the studio and chatting to the celebs, as they love giving their opinions on things and hopefully wouldn't send me anywhere grim. I couldn't do all this in a day, so decided to start with the furthest point and get the ferry across to Manly. The views across the harbour were breath-taking, and I finally realised how huge the harbour bridge was and how weird the Opera House looked. I probably used an entire disposable camera just getting there! The choppy blue water and spray in my face was the most refreshing feeling ever and I felt so free. Free from dance hold with Trent, free from constantly trying to impress the producers, and free from always trying to look perfect in case Miss Universe's boyfriend accidentally glanced my way and decided he wanted to marry me. I realised a bit of time on my own and away from people did me good. When I reached Manly, I didn't even do that much. I strolled up and

down the boardwalk in awe of all the volleyball courts and skilled players, the impressive surfers, cute dogs and how it was much more normal to carry a surfboard under your arm than a handbag. What a vibe!

It was there that I tried sushi for the first time. It was everywhere in Australia, and I wanted to stick to my travelling rule of only eating things I couldn't get back home, or just weren't easy to get. I sat on a bench overlooking the ocean and cracked open my little box of Japanese delights. I was hooked! As well as a mini fish-shaped soy sauce bottle, it also had a tiny sachet of green, thick sauce. If this was the world's smallest portion of guacamole, I'd be bitterly disappointed... So I squeezed the entire packet out into a big blob onto my chopsticks and gobbled it up. It took a few seconds to kick in, as it was pretty tasteless initially, and then the heat came. I started cooing like an injured owl as I believed I'd just ingested actual fire. The old man on the bench next to mine looked at me as if I were some kind of deranged bird woman, and promptly left, walking as fast as he could in the opposite direction. To this day, I always pass on wasabi sauce now that I know it's literally Satan's condiment.

Somehow, I think the blast of heat affected my brain as well as my taste buds, because I completely forgot to check the last ferry time. I had lost track of time all together and was even contemplating staying to watch the sunset. (I'm a sucker for pink sky.) I saw a ferry pull into the port and thought, "Nah, I'll get the next one." For whatever reason, something prompted me to ask a stranger when the last ferry was.

"It's that one that's leaving now, mate."

"No! Wait!" I screamed in my head, as I legged it down the path and miraculously made it. As much as I was enjoying sitting on that bench, I didn't fancy sleeping on it.

The next ferry wasn't until 8 a.m. the next morning. It all worked out great, as I got to watch the sunset from the boat and then admire the stars as nightfall quickly descended. How lovely. Until the biggest creep on the boat decided to hone in on me, telling me he could "show me a good time" and "did I like to party?"

"No thanks mate, I'm actually very boring," I answered, swiftly moving away to the other side of the boat. He appeared beside me again, telling me I was beautiful and asking me to accompany him to the best bars in town.

"Ermm No! I'm only 17 and I only drink water or smoothies."

"That's okay. I know places I can get you into," he replied, creepily.

Eww no! He must have been about 40 and probably didn't mind what beverage I had, as long as there was something for him to slip the Rohypnol into. I started to panic inside and spent the entire twilight ferry trip running round the upper deck trying to get away from him. But I couldn't. I was on a flippin' boat! This right here is a prime example of why I don't want to be stuck on a cruise ship with Trent as a show skater.

In the end, I literally started blanking him. Don't engage!! But not even that made him stop following me with his pervy comments. I knew I needed to plan my escape route and I decided to jump in the first taxi I saw when I legged it off the boat, regardless of whether or not anyone was in it. I managed to push my way to the front as everyone funnel necked down the fold out walkway to land. He was calling after me to come back but I didn't give him a second glance. I kept my eyes frantically scanning the car park for a taxi. And there one was! I leapt inside and yelled, "Drive please!"

The poor driver jumped out of his skin, and I explained I was escaping from a creepy guy. Without any questions he hit the gas and was more than happy to act as my getaway driver. He told me to be careful as there were a lot of weirdos about, always trying to pick up young girls like me, with the offer of free drinks and exclusive mystery venues. What perverts!

Anyway, I arrived home in one piece, albeit a lot later than planned, and to a very worried Carol. I reassured her everything had gone perfectly and the only hitch in my day was the killer wasabi. I didn't want to worry her or for her to forbid me going out tomorrow for phase two of exploring. I knew I'd be fine and was sure I'd have more luck with the koalas.

Chapter 19 – Try Everything Once

Let's be honest: it's not hard to blow all your spends in a short space of time while travelling. Especially when you're trying to fit everything in before being trapped on a 19-hour flight home. My last remaining days in Sydney were a huge success! I zipped across the harbour in water taxis, went to the zoo and stroked baby koalas and kangaroos, took a cable car, avoided ALL wasabi, took a tour of Sydney Opera House, consumed a lot of fro-yo, and went through many disposable cameras. I decided not to do the climb of Sydney Harbour Bridge. Although I love heights, I didn't really have the time or budget and it would mostly be full of couples proposing to one another.

On my last trip to the studio, I made the most of hanging with the final celebs in the green room, and managed to scale down my last interaction with Trent to just practising lifts off ice. I figured it would be the last time I was twirled around that high above a guy's head in a while. And, it was safer to drop the bomb off ice rather than on, when I told him "It's been fun and all, but I think you should find another girl to go into shows with. BYE!"

I said my farewells to everyone with a bittersweet feeling in my heart. I'd had an amazing time but knew I most likely wouldn't see any of my new Australian friends again, unless it was in a magazine.

On the way home, I'd arranged to spend a couple of days in Dubai with my mum's goddaughter. This was a genius idea, as it broke the journey up for me and I got to see another new country. It was the height of summer, though, and at 52 degrees, you'd spend your life running from air-conditioned mall to air-conditioned car to air-conditioned home. You simply couldn't be outside, and coming straight from lush, green, outdoorsy, surf-mad

Sydney, this was a shock to the system. Who in their right mind opens their oven door, inhales the burning air and goes, "Wow! I really want to go on holiday there!" That's what it was like. I actually spent most of my time sleeping as I was severely jet lagged, and the only thing I recall doing was trying to barter on a market stall for a fake designer handbag, then walking away because I didn't understand the currency. Or eating Arabic bread on the beach in the evening, when it was slightly less like breathing in fire. It was good to be able to get off the plane for 48 hours, but I was happy to leave this glorified sandpit with its many construction cranes, and couldn't understand why anyone would want to go back.

I spent the rest of British summertime throwing myself into driving lessons. I got a new instructor who looked just like comedian Peter Kay and he was great. Even if he didn't have a purple car. I passed first time with flying colours and the first place I drove myself to was the gym later that evening. I felt like the coolest girl in the world! Especially when I offered to give my brother a lift somewhere on the way. He was always trying to get one up on me with his many scientific facts and condescending tones, but despite having A-Level Biology, did he know how to work a clutch? No! He showed no interest in learning to drive, although he was old enough, but it was probably safer for everyone if he didn't, as his hand eye coordination was terrible and he struggled with catching a ball.

I gradually started filling mum's car with pink fluffy accessories: pink fluffy steering wheel cover, 'Babe on board' sign, pink mats, a Hello Kitty mirror muff, headrest covers, and a pink feather boa along the back window, which cleverly made it look like you were wearing it around your shoulders if you sat in the back. In hindsight, it probably looked like a brothel on wheels. But I didn't care that I looked like a stereotypical, pink obsessed, newbie girl racer. I adored driving and pink things. Mum on the other hand, would cower into her seat in embarrassment at traffic lights, while vans full of young lads would creep forward, craning their necks to check her out. Maybe expecting someone slightly younger. Who knows? She had the patience of a saint to let me have my fun and use her car as if it was my own. I called it 'Mary' and the previous model she had was Joseph. The next one would have probably been baby Jesus, but we never got that far.

With driving comes freedom and I would regularly take myself on little drives in big circles around the local area. I'd blast my tunes, even if it meant I couldn't hear my clutch bite point and generally try to attract as much attention to myself as possible. I wasn't particularly trusted to do long motorway drives, so Mum would drive me to any auditions further afield or the occasional Blackburn trip. I wasn't skating that much as I was just doing the necessary hours for my coaching training. The rest of the time, it was auditions or spraying people on the shop floor at Rackhams. I'd not been with my current agent that long, so I was slightly taken aback when they rang me to say I had an audition for a new character on popular sitcom 'Hollyoaks', in two days' time. This potentially could be huge! Riding high on my recent success of having just played a lead role in a BBC comedy drama, Channel 4 may well want to snap me up next right?!

When I rocked up there, I soon realised there was a definite Hollyoaks 'look', and that I didn't have it: Long blonde hair, fake boobs, fake nails, fake tan. I didn't know anything about the character I was auditioning for, other than she was called "Debbie". Until they handed me the script... I was auditioning for a prostitute. My heart sank. I didn't want to do that! I knew there and then I wasn't going to get the part, even before I stepped foot in the audition room. As more and more girls were piled into the holding area, I started to feel like a sheep, rammed on one of those awful lorries on its way to market. I was already sweating as it was the hottest day ever and they were ramming us into the tiniest waiting room with no windows. I waited hours to be called in, knowing this was going to be a waste of time but putting it all down to experience. I'm sure there would be a lot more days like this, although hopefully with less of the sweaty, fake-tan smell.

I was so glad to get out of there. I didn't get a callback or indeed the part, but the girl who did went on to marry a guy from boy band Westlife, so I couldn't help but think what my life would've been like if I could channel my inner hooker.

My next audition was at the other end of the scale: a theatre audition for the role of Beth in Little Women in London's West End. For a girl with no formal acting training, this was also a tall order. I tried my best but was a little confused why the guy reading opposite me was so overly animated. It was weirdly distracting as all the auditions I'd done up till now, the person reading the other character is usually purposefully deadpan. This guy would even jump up out of his seat at times! It was only as I was leaving, feeling like I'd far from nailed it, that I realised, "That's theatre darling!" Completely different from the TV acting technique I had been used to.

I had much to learn (clearly), so I decided to book myself onto an evening 'Acting for Theatre' course at The University of Manchester, followed by the 'Acting for Television' course that started straight after it.

I quit my fragrance job at Rackhams even before I had a coaching job in the bag. You'll see I have a habit of doing that. Leaving something to make space for the next thing, although I might not have it in place yet. If the next step of life was within my sights, I'd make the leap, truly believing it would work out, even if I couldn't tell you how. This can make for a few nail-biting weeks of uncertainty as you fall into that 'in-between phase', but I'd passed all written parts of my ice-skating coaching and was confident I'd pass the practical. I did. With distinction! So, I found myself working at the new ice rink in Altrincham.

Like a personal trainer starting at a new gym, I had to build a client base and pay my rent to work there, even if I'd not earned it. The other coaches were immediately hostile towards me. Many of them worked at the original rink and remembered me when I was nine years old and just learning. Now, here I was, the new coach on the scene, the youngest one there by about 50 years and the fear of me poaching their pupils was a reality. They'd complain about where I parked my car in the staff car park, which seat I put my bag under in the coach's room and even resorted to trapping me and my pupils, as they'd make their group circle mine, leaving us marooned in the centre of the ice. It was pathetic.

When I looked around at my fellow coaches, I saw how miserable they all were. All tired, cold, guzzling black coffee, living their lives in ski wear and constantly harassed by pushy parents and skater mums. Many of them were steeped in resentment they had their competitive careers cut short due to injury or lack of partner. Or their show careers cut short because they got too fat and were released from the cast. (It happens). Did any of them actually look happy? No. Did I really want to follow in their footsteps and be that miserable old coach? Standing there, freezing, grunting, "Do it again." Or "Great, but try not to fall"? No! Everything inside me was screaming it. But this was meant to be my career. This was what everyone expected of me. I was 18 years old and earning £30 an hour but I wasn't happy. My dad always said, "If you're not happy doing what you're doing, you're not getting paid enough." Something I strongly disagree with. That's like saying money and happiness are the same thing. They're really not. Money buys you freedom, not happiness. And the way I was feeling, I was pretty sure you could pay me triple that per hour and I still wouldn't enjoy teaching people repeatedly how to get up after they fall, or skater mum's ringing me at 10 p.m. on a Sunday night.

I had to plan my escape and I was pinning all my hopes on my acting career. What better excuse for calling it a day in a once-dreamed-about career than getting a big role in a TV show and spending my 6 a.m. to 7 a.m. in the make-up truck, instead of the frosty coaches' room?!

I changed agents as this one wasn't doing anything for me. I consulted Caroline and once again, she offered some real pearls of wisdom. This new agency hadn't been around too long but already had some big names on their books and a run of successful bookings. They immediately thought I'd make a great Disney girl and sent me for new, brighter, smiley headshots to channel my inner Disney Princess. This was more like it! No boob job or slutiness required. The new headshots worked, and within a week I was sent for my first big audition with them. Low and behold, it was for the Disney Channel! One minute I'm at the ice rink hating children, the next, I'm on a train to London, blasting Taylor Swift in my headphones. This was much more my scene.

All the other girls in the audition holding area were similar to me, really friendly, and one had even brought her mum with her as she'd never auditioned for anything before and needed the moral support. (Sweet!) It also gave me a confidence boost knowing my CV was clearly much stronger than hers. Like most castings, it went in the blink of an eye, but I felt great afterwards and strolled down Carnaby Street to sit in my favourite juice bar, before jumping on the train home.

I ended up getting called back TWICE and shortlisted for the final three. They were struggling to choose between me and one other girl, so they wrote in an additional character that they made me read for. After meeting the Executive Producer, top-of-the-food-chain guy and he's saying things like, "Sophie! Great to meet you! I've heard a lot about you..." Naturally, it got my hopes up. They skyrocketed in fact, and I was already rehearsing my "I'm leaving to pursue a TV career with Disney" speech to Head Coach David and all the annoying parents.

Like any actress will know, when you hear, it's usually because you've got the part. When you don't, forget it ever happened, don't dwell on your failure. Move on. For me, sitting at home picking my nails on the date the show starts shooting is usually a good indication. The crushing realisation sets in that you came so frustratingly close to your life changing and here you are, back to square one, like a game of Snakes and Ladders. Oh, and in case you're wondering, the girl who got the part was the one who'd never auditioned for anything before. That began to teach me that it's not necessarily the most experienced girl who gets the role. It's a lot about how you look and even more about who you know.

I wish I could say my 18-year-old self was still able to enjoy the normal fun things that most other 18-year-olds were experiencing, but in reality, I couldn't be out late or go out at the weekends. I was on the ice at 6 a.m. to teach two hours of free lessons to pay my rent. The only thing I'd be getting dressed up to go out in was ski wear and a fleece headband to keep my ears warm. I was living just like the 50-year-old coaches, minus the black coffee and knee replacement from a lifetime of knee bends. (Although I was getting that way.) I would blow most of my wages on weekly spray tans and blow dries, even though the only place I went was the ice rink or my living room.

Two more big auditions followed but these ones I got entirely off my own back. I was contacted by a casting director I'd met on a one-off acting workshop. She'd remembered me and wanted me to audition for a new BBC series about a girl who was just like me, with her quest and dreams of fame! I fit the brief perfectly, besides having to put on a Yorkshire accent. If a casting director likes you and brings you in, you're already halfway there. I felt like the stars were aligning and I was once again rehearsing my leaving speech and emails to all my ice-rink colleagues. The hopes sprung high and several agonising weeks of callback auditions and general waiting and praying passed, until I get a personal phone call from casting director Jenny. She was so impressed with me and really liked me. The whole team did. But they'd chosen another girl because they felt I was just 'too pretty'. Too pretty? Are you kidding me? You should see me in the morning with no makeup! Or when I've squeezed puss out of my pores and they go all red and lumpy on my face! I felt like I couldn't win in this game.

Time to change tactics. I signed up to one of those casting websites where they post all kinds of weird and wonderful jobs and auditions. It was there that I saw a casting for a new reality style show with one of the biggest 'It' girls of the moment, both here and in the States, Paris Hilton's British Best Friend.

I know what most people were thinking: that sounds horrific. And yes, you're probably right, and being put in a house with twelve other girls all trying to impress Paris is a disaster waiting to happen! I was always very anti Big Brother and similar shows, but this was different. The tasks would involve accompanying her to glitzy events and fun girly activities for eight weeks, with the final three getting flown to LA to battle it out for the ultimate lifestyle prize. This is what hooked me in. I'd grown utterly obsessed with LA and Hollywood in particular, and I saw this whole contrived, mentally unstimulating show as a potential way in. I'd already spent hours in the past researching flights, hotels, neighbourhoods and hotspots, only to come up against the same problem: I had to be over 21 (Damn!) to go on my own. Getting to the final on this show would fix all that, no doubt flying the finalists on business class, and what better person to hang out with while there than the current queen of Hollywood: Paris Hilton. I wrote my punchiest application form, detailing all my random and unconventional life experiences, and why I think I'd make a great best friend for good old Paris. An ice-skater-turned-actress from Manchester, with a love for travel and talent for shopping in dollars, was just what she needed! I got accepted to attend the first round of auditions straight away and threw on some leopard print, skinny jeans and my highest heels, before heading to the then-Granada studios in Manchester. That alone was exciting as it's where they filmed Coronation Street and many other big shows. Who knows who I might pass in the corridor or meet in the loo?

It was cut-throat from the get-go as we were grouped together and put in a massive circle, about 30 of us. After the initial "Stand up and tell us an interesting fact about yourself," we then had to say who in the group we were least likely to be friends with. Ouch! I barely knew any of these people 20 minutes ago and I really didn't want to judge anyone so quickly off a rushed first impression. The others, however, wasted no time at all in giving each other a grilling, with the second girl they asked choosing me to lay into.

"I'm least likely to be friends with you. Sorry, who are you again? Sophie? Yeah, you. Because my dad's an ice hockey coach and if I hear any more about ice skating, I might just kill myself," she sneered.

Wow, okay. Maybe a little strong but naturally I replied with an, "Oh sorry. That's okay, then, I understand!" As if I had anything to apologise for.

Suddenly the producers started blasting Katy Perry's 'I Kissed a Girl' loudly, and asked us all to take it in turns to pretend we were walking down a red carpet, then pose for the paparazzi. I couldn't wait for my turn! I'd been practising this since I was eight. It was like a budding singer being handed a mic for the first time after years of holding a hairbrush. I felt like a strong candidate until out of nowhere, another brunette burst into the room, shrieking.

"Oh my God I'm so sorry I'm late! I crashed my car! I nearly died for Paris! Anyway, I'm here now. Hiya. Hi! Hi everyone! Sorry, where should I sit?" she said, in a kind of verbal diarrhoea and the strongest Scouse accent. She looked a lot like me but prettier and with better hair. As she tossed the longest weave extensions over her shoulder and stumbled to her seat, I began to wonder how she could even drive in the enormous strappy wedge platforms she was wearing. Thankfully she was okay, and she definitely made an entrance, I'll give her that.

Moments later, the team of execs and producers announced they would been sending us all home from this round apart from five of us. The person announced first was clumsy but lovable late Scouse girl, followed by the flamboyant gay guy in the homemade Paris Hilton T shirt. I could see how this was going to go. I wasn't loud enough, bitchy enough or wild enough for this show.

"And... Sophie Wright" they called lastly, snapping me out of my defeatist thoughts. While the others were quickly ushered out, I was called up first to the next stage and was brought into a dimly lit boardroom with the three executives sat at one end, and little me, on the one lone chair, way at the other end. It felt like being in the boardroom on The Apprentice or being interrogated for a crime I didn't commit. They were brutal. They fired questions at me from every angle, twisting what I said, putting words in my mouth and trying to catch me out at every opportunity. I was proud of myself for holding my own and keeping cool under pressure, safe in the knowledge my leopard-print top was disguising my sweat patches. I skipped home that day feeling like there was still hope for me, despite not being savagely cutthroat and genuinely just wanting a free flight to LA.

I ended up getting a callback. Several in fact. And I made it down to the final 30, almost making it into the house.

My final audition was the most catty and intense of all. Me and two other girls were sat in a triangle, where they'd literally try to start a fight amongst us, making us say what we didn't like about one another. I hated this. I hated confrontation and was paranoid about upsetting anyone, even if it was detrimental to myself. I was achingly diplomatic and resorted to gently telling the next girl I liked her, but didn't like her makeup. That she had such lovely eyes, but if she did her eyeliner slightly differently it would accentuate them much more. Then I winced inside hoping I'd not hurt her. The others wasted no time in telling me how annoyingly happy I was or hated my jazzy fashion tights – although so on-trend at the time. We then got interviewed separately about what we would do to backstab the next person, and then had more pictures taken of us. I had to sign several forms and was told under no circumstances was I to tell anyone about the show or what I was here auditioning for before it aired. Top secret. OK, got it.

On my way to the exit, I passed one of the other auditionees interrogating the most terrified young runner. He was so nervous and was desperately trying not to look at her boobs. I remembered her from the first audition. She was fierce and was the oldest girl there. She was mercilessly grilling him about when would she find out, and that they "had better put her in the show, or else!" She would have got on great with the Mother Mafia at the rink and was destined to be one, I'm sure. If she didn't become a Paris's 'best friend' first. I was ushered out through another exit round the back. The same one that all the famous Coronation Street actors come and go by. There were always groups of superfans and paparazzi hanging round there all day. I felt a million dollars in my outfit and new trench coat, channelling Kate Moss, so I welcomed all the superfans staring at me through the bars, while I waited for the security guard to buzz me out. I smiled at them as I began to totter past them carefully on my heels across the cobbles.

"What were you doing in there?" one asked.

"Are you the new barmaid on Coronation Street?" another beamed.

With what I'd just been told still ringing in my ears, to NOT divulge any information, I simply replied "Erm, I'm not allowed to say..."

"It's her!" another one shouted, and before I could blink, the whole group had descended around me, shoving their note pads in my face and holding out cameras towards me.

"To 'Michael' please," a man asked excitedly.

"Can mine be to 'Amy'"? another called. I didn't have the heart to tell them I wasn't whoever they thought I was, so I went along with it.

"Sure!" I politely obliged, doing my prettiest signature, complete with a little star dotting the I and a love heart curl on the S. I did feel a bit bad, but I obviously looked like a star and I certainly felt like one, the way I was so simply making their day with my Sharpie squiggles.

"So when will we be seeing you on the small screen?"

"Oh, you'll have to wait and see... But keep watching!" I replied, cryptically. I was getting the hang of this! They thanked me and I thanked them as I came up for air, walking away having completed my signings. As I walked towards my dad's Mondeo that was there to collect me (wishing it was the blacked-out Mercedes van), a man from the group ran in front of me then started running backwards, whipping out a massive camera and blinding me with the repeated flashes. He was paparazzi! It was happening. I was getting paparazzi'd! I quickly engaged my brain, breaking into a strut, smile and wave as I headed towards the car, at which point, out of nowhere, another one jumped out of a bush and started snapping away too. Two of them. This was really happening! As I surprisingly (to them) jumped in the old grey Mondeo, they snapped a few last shots of me through the window as my dad drove off.

"DID YOU SEE THAT?!" I squealed, "I just got paparazzi'd! It finally happened! I shall remember this day forever!"

I was kind of frustrated that dad seemed to have no reaction and just went, "So how did the audition go?" in his deadpan tone.

"WHO CARES ABOUT THE AUDITION! I just got papped!" If that wasn't a good omen, I don't know what is.

When the show finally aired, I realised I'd dodged the biggest bullet ever. The others in the contestant's house would have made mincemeat out of me. There were cameras everywhere, nasty pranks being played and they were all portrayed as the worst and dumbest of humanity. I probably wouldn't have pooed for a week, and slept with one eye open for fear of losing an eyebrow. Most worryingly of all, no one would have taken me seriously as an actress if I had made it onto that show. Of all the contestants there was one pretty, northern brunette girl... It was (you guessed it) the car-crashing, entrance- making, ditsy but lovable Scouse girl. She ended up quitting after the first two weeks and I couldn't help thinking most of these people would be psychologically scarred in some way after this. I, on the other hand, managed to convince a hoard of Corrie superfans that I was in fact the new barmaid, got paparazzi'd, enjoyed several trips to the famous Granada studios and relished the opportunity to audition for something where the only thing I had to be was myself. Maybe that was the route I should be going down? Just be myself.

Like after any audition, the mundane everyday life goes on and you slot back into it, trying not to dwell on the fact you nearly made it onto something and instead, try to keep your life as exciting as possible. Lucky for me, things were never normal, and my weekends suddenly became very exciting indeed.

Chapter 20 – Ice, Camera, Action!

Celebrities on Ice was into its second series and the budget and ratings were set to be bigger than ever. Carol was once again on the judging panel, head coach and responsible for auditioning the celebrities and their partners. She knew I was in a bit of a rut again, not loving coaching little kids and being hated by most other coaches, and still not on a big TV series. When she threw the idea out there of me auditioning for the show, skating with a celebrity on prime-time national TV, being immediately thrust into that glittering world, I was practically kissing her feet already for merely suggesting the idea. Like anything, I'd have to be judged, scrutinised, auditioned and prove my worth, but despite me being just 18 and all the other professionals in their mid to late-30s, I had so much experience and so much to offer.

I needed to submit an audition tape showcasing my best moves and biggest lifts, so Carol hooked me up with her star pro show skater 'David' for an hour. My mum filmed take after take with our ancient camcorder and her shaky hands, as David swung me round repeatedly by various limbs, above his head, through his legs and anything else impressive looking we could think of. I was like a human ragdoll and felt like I'd been hit by a truck afterwards. I ended up with two black eyes and burst blood vessels due to all the centrifugal force. When I mentioned it to Carol, she brushed it off saying, "Yeah, that's David for you, he has a tendency to spin girls too fast!" Great. Heavy duty concealer required then, and a huge appreciation for the fact my teeth were still intact.

It didn't stop there though; I ended up nannying the CEO's two kids during pre-production, while they were over for two weeks from the States. This was not my forte, looking after a 6 and 8-year-old, but I did it. Carol strongly recommended it, as it would help me get into the "inner circle." Whatever this mystical inner circle was, I wanted to be in it. If it would get me in a CEO's good books and prove my work ethic, thus making me a more desirable choice for the show, I'd look after as many hyperactive kids as you want. I knew things were hard work when one of the kids said to the other, "Becky, have you had your medication today?" I think it was me that needed medication after that two weeks. And maybe a short spell of therapy. I reasoned with myself that this was far better than having to sleep with someone to get a roll, something I promised myself I would never do.

The 'waiting to find out' was positively sickening, and I couldn't think or talk about anything else. I was constantly asking Carol for updates and sometimes she'd be annoyingly vague. Until one day, mum had a freakishly vivid dream... She dreamt I was on the show with a popular, young and handsome X Factor runner up. We became the nation's sweethearts over the course of the show, ended up winning it and then rode through the whole set on a steam roller! Bringing a whole new meaning to the term 'smashing it'. She couldn't get it out of her head, so she rang Carol to share it with her.

Carol fell silent on the phone, possibly thinking mum was crazy but then came out with "I don't believe this... I have just auditioned him this morning! How did you know?" she squeaked, in total shock. Mum didn't know, obviously, but she had always been a bit psychic. Apparently, he was great and would be the perfect height, style and age to partner with me.

I felt like all the planets were aligning. Surely this was meant to be? He was the youngest celebrity by a mile, I'd be the youngest pro by a mile, and to put him with anyone else would look like he was dancing with his mum. More weeks of agonising waiting passed, and Carol became more and more distant. The feeling of doubt in me started to fester but also the feeling of hope. Although looking back, it was sheer desperation. I wanted this more than anything and I was in too deep for this simply not to happen. All the signs were there! This should be it. I got black eyes for this, was Carol's star pupil, and on paper and in reality, I was a perfect fit.

In the end, one of the producer's interns rang me. I think Carol put him up to it because she didn't have the balls to tell me herself. They weren't going to have me on the show. They felt I was too young and maybe wouldn't cope. Wouldn't cope? I'd already lived away from home on an intense filming schedule, trained for years, won titles, put up with idiotic partners, was unfazed by celebrities, early starts, hard work, loved being in front of a camera and could more than take every bit of this in my stride! I was devastated they didn't see it that way. Did they even see me? See my demo tape? And why the hell didn't Carol fight for me more? Was I even in the running or did she do this just to get me excited and motivated for skating again? She could sell sand to the Arabs, and I knew if she'd have stuck her neck out for me a bit, they would have chosen me. She must have felt slightly bad because when the show began, she sorted it so that Mum and I could be in the studio audience each week with the VIPs. It definitely softened the blow, as suddenly people would actually see my weekly spray tan and blow dry outside of Altrincham Ice rink, and I would live for the weekend road trip to London. Knocking around a TV studio where they once filmed Star Wars and currently filmed Big Brother was just the type of weekend I needed. Even if the Big Brother house did look like a shed in real life. You never knew who you might run into. Either on the row behind yours or the studio bar that everyone would pile into afterwards. Where you'd rub shoulders with all the stars and their even starrier friends. It was here where I had several encounters with people who could potentially sway my life one way or another...

Every week the crowd seemed to get more star studded than the last. Imagine a mix of has-been but still well-loved pop stars, current soap stars, models, sporting legends and the biggest names in TV all squished into a long narrow bar, all trying to get a drink. We were all parched and starving after three hours of whooping, clapping, stand up, sit down, laughing or any other commands we were given as audience members. I was literally rubbing shoulders with my teenage heartthrobs and often surprised at how normal, scruffy or short they were in real life.

Occasionally I'd want the ground to swallow me up, though, when Mum would say highly inappropriate things without realizing it. Like when I got talking to Duncan from boy band Blue. I was trying to play it cool, but she went, "Isn't she gorgeous, my lovely daughter?! 18 - untouched by human hands!" she exclaimed, brimming with pride. Duncan coughed out his drink, almost choking and managed an "Erm yes, she's lovely", not knowing where to look. Mum was my biggest cheerleader and was always trying to marry me off to the first eligible male, but I had to have a word after that. No oversharing moments, please. Especially not in front of heart throb boy band members.

Sometimes it was the other party putting their foot in it however, making comments about me which I felt were inappropriate, in general, not just with my mum present. Like the week the creative director of the world's largest touring ice show and his choreographer husband were there. They were good friends and former colleagues of Carol so naturally we got talking. He'd heard a lot about me from her and basically offered me a place in the cast of his famous cruise ship show. An opportunity most skaters would tread over anyone for, and to be asked by the man himself is like a golden ticket. No one says no to this guy. Ever. But there I was, trying to be as diplomatic as possible and politely decline. I was starting to waffle when his flamboyant husband came over.

"Darling! This is Sophie, the ice dancer Carol was telling us about."

"Mmm Mmm! Now that is a nice piece of meat!" he blurted out. "Give us a twirl, honey! Oh yes, very nice, we could definitely use that!"

I let out a shy, nervous laugh and (I hate to say it) did an awkward twirl. Mum was less than impressed that some random guy had just referred to her daughter as a 'piece of meat'. Awkward.

"I know, darling. I've just offered her a place in the production but she's telling me she doesn't want it", he snapped. (Even more awkward).

"Honestly, I'm so flattered you would ask me personally, but I'm happy coaching" (lie). "And want to focus on pursuing my acting career" (true).

"You're wasted coaching!" he barked. "Look, the offer's there if you want it, and most girls would kill for this opportunity..." (awkward levels peaking now).

Before I could come back with a response, he turned on his heels and headed off for more champagne, while his husband quickly followed. Mum and I threw each other a look, knowing exactly what one another was thinking. Can we go back to her pimping me out to boy band members, please?

Thankfully, I didn't have to wait long for the kind of opportunity I actually wanted to come my way...

This came in the form of soap star hunk and all-round bad boy, 'Jamie Hart'. Living up to his reputation both on and off screen, he was very tipsy and made no secret of the fact I had caught his eye.

"Well, hello there! What's your name?" he asked loudly, suddenly stopping his drunken laddish dancing and sauntering right up into my personal body space. His face lit up when I told him I was one of Carol's skaters and now a budding actress. He was a couple of years older than me, and on one of the most popular soap operas on TV, thanks to his magic touch of an agent, who was right there getting sozzled with him. He was heavily flirting and I was pinching myself, while growing increasingly concerned about my sweaty upper lip. Tipsiness aside, we were getting on great and he seemed genuine in wanting to help me in the acting world, as well as date me. I was happy with both of these things! Suddenly, this random woman stumbled over who I thought was his mum and draped herself around him. It was in fact his agent, who he'd just been telling me about.

"I owe it all to this woman!" he gushed. "You two should talk. This is Sophie, she's an actress too, done a TV series and she skates... Sign her up Kate!" he shouted, as he got pulled away from us into a cluster of his yobbish mates.

It was the best intro ever and immediately opened up the conversation to business talk. (Sell yourself Sophie!) I told her all about my show and all my achievements and she was keen. Despite being tipsy, although I'm sure that helped, she reached into her handbag and gave me her card.

"Call me and come into my office for a chat this week."

Result! As I thanked her and tried not to get too giddy, I glanced down at the name on the card... 'Kate Hornby', it read. That's when I had the biggest realisation yet. This was THE Kate Hornby; responsible for half the bright young stars in our most loved soaps, the agent whose books every young actor is trying to get on! She's known for having the magic formula for making TV stars and had a direct 'in' with all the biggest casting directors. Not only that, she runs an acting school in the north that churns out superstar after superstar. Somewhere any young actor would sell an organ just to get on the wait list for. But the most incredible thing of all was that I had applied to train there and be represented by her just a few weeks back. After doing my research of all current actors I wanted to be like and follow in their footsteps, I discovered it was her who discovered them all.

"Wait...," I croaked. "You're Kate Hornby? THE Kate Hornby ?"

"Yes!" she laughed.

"Kate Hornby of the award-winning acting school, and agent to half of soap land Kate Hornby!?" I shrieked. I couldn't play it cool at this point, that ship had long sailed.

"That's me, yes!" she laughed again, giving me a big hug. A hug. And her personal phone number. We are practically mates now! I explained how I had been following her work and her talent, and had even applied to the school but was still waiting to hear back.

"Oh, there's always a huge backlog! Anyway, you've got my number now. Call me Monday." And off she went. To grab another bottle of Blue Wicked and hold Jamie's legs while he precariously danced on a chair. What an amazing encounter! I couldn't believe what had just happened and what a small world it was. How I'd suddenly found myself getting hit on by a celebrity and introduced to his agent, who was interested in me! I guarded that card with my life and the only thing that could've made that night better would be if Jamie had asked for my number. There was time for that, though. Especially now we could be sharing the same agent as well as the same skating coach. Life works in mysterious ways.

I honestly could not have given a shit about coaching at this point. There were far more exciting things going on, and I just used it as a means of paying for my weekly blow dries and spray tans. As long as I looked good at the TV studio and kept rubbing shoulders with the right people, I'd be out of here in no time.

Later that week, as promised, I had my meeting with Kate. I loved how chilled she was, dressed super casual and glugging a Starbucks. She had high hopes for me and promptly bypassed me on the waiting list and requested I start attending the weekly classes at her acting school straight away. I could just about afford it, thanks to my boring but necessary coaching job. And besides, it was worth every penny for Kate to see me perform and hone my craft every week in her workshop. It was her name above the door and she's the person everyone wanted to impress. There was one small problem, though...

"Can we rough it up a bit?" She asked. "You're a bit clean cut and there's not many roles like that for young girls. Could you do Shameless?

For those of you who are unaware, Shameless is as dire as it sounds. Loved by many for how vile, vulgar and horrific it is, it's set on a council estate in Manchester and portrays the very worst of humanity. Sex, drugs, alcoholism, abuse, crime, benefits fraud – you name it, if it was shameful enough, it would be on that show. It's about as far away from the Disney Channel as I could get.

"I guess so! If that's what the role required," I blurted out. "I'd just need to build up to it though." I knew full well I was never going to simulate sex on TV, do any nudity or play a chav, but if Kate saw me each week in class, she'd soon see

I was better suited to other roles. Preferably a classy new girl written into Coronation Street or a period drama maybe. Sign me up! I should have been more excited when I left, but on the journey home all that kept ringing in my ears was "Can we rough it up a bit?" Really not what I wanted to hear, leaving me with a sense of self-doubt growing inside me. Was I really cut out for this? I snapped myself out of it and reminded myself I must be on the right path. This whole in-road with Kate wouldn't have happened like this if it wasn't meant to be, right?

Annoyingly, Carol couldn't get us tickets for the show that week. I didn't mind too much as we'd been going most weekends, and it was probably time her own daughters took advantage of the tickets for once. What pissed me off more than anything was when she told me Jamie had been pestering her for my number at training, and she told him 'NO'. And to keep away from me, I'm 'not his sort of girl'. What the actual hell?! I was furious with her. She failed to get me on the show after building my hopes up so high, the very least she could do was give a celebrity my number who might actually take me out for dinner, get me signed to his agent, then probably get papped together and be on the cover of Heat magazine with the headline, "Mystery girl steals Jamie's Hart." For God's sake Carol, why can you not see this? I'm not sure what the female equivalent of "cock-blocking" was. As much as I hate that term, that's exactly what she did.

As time went on, I began to realise it was utterly pointless waiting and hoping that someone would give you an opportunity or a leg up in some way. 'If you want something doing, do it yourself' has never been a more accurate saying. My so-called agent seemed to had forgotten I existed, and I hadn't heard from her in weeks. I started attending Kate's acting workshop but was seriously underwhelmed to find she was hardly ever there, and the type of people that were, were like fame hungry understudies for the Shameless cast if it ever got made into a stage show. They were all VERY rough around the edges and not particularly friendly. There was only one other girl that really spoke to me, and she was new too. She was based in London and was going to get the train up every week and staying in a hotel, just so she could attend here each week. Expensive! But she was doing it gladly because, like me, she'd heard about Kate and her magical acting school factory for churning out superstars. Despite all the hype surrounding this place, she too was majorly unimpressed. The same old same old exercises each week and still no appearance from Kate herself.

Very quickly we were put into small groups of four or five, then tasked with writing our own short sketch or play to perform at a showcase in a local theatre in one month's time. I'm no playwright so this wasn't really what I'd signed up for. To make this even more irritating, we were then told there would be no classes or teaching as such before the showcase, but we were still required to come in at the same time each week and rehearse. This was a massive cop out in my opinion. What exactly am I paying for here? A harshly lit room full of massive egos? Sorry, no, a small space in the corner of a big room, two plastic chairs to act as a bench or sofa, and a lot of other desperate and dramatic people getting in your way, was a more accurate description.

Living in the hope that I'd be skipping into the rink to quit by telling them I'd scored myself a role in Coronation Street was looking seriously doubtful. I was putting all my eggs firmly in that one basket, thinking that it would give me an easy out for jacking in my skating career and no one would blame me for it. If life would make the decision for me, it would save me having to say my real reason for leaving: that I simply wasn't happy. I was in pain with my knees from spending everyday teaching beginners 'lemons'. My back was bad from leaning down to hold up little ones or worse, holding up terrified, ungainly adults who saw me as a human rail to cling onto, cutting off the circulation in my arm as they squeezed it blue with terror.

My alien hands and circulation problem got worse for spending so many hours just standing in a freezing environment. It took me till Thursday to earn my rent if nobody cancelled and it was due Sunday morning. Most of the other coaches still had a weird issue with me and hostile attitude. Half the kids didn't want to be there; it was their pushy parent's dream. And above all: I hated ski wear.

But life doesn't cut you that kind of slack when it comes to making decisions. It purposefully won't make it easy for you because it forces you to do those things you really don't want to do. You need to learn from them, you need to experience them. Clearly, it needed me to feel the fear but do it anyway. Half my life spent on ice. Years, hours, blood, sweat, tears, to then pack it all in despite having no job to go onto, no acting gig in the bag and a wardrobe full of thermals. What would people think? What would they say to me or about me? I'm telling you now, it doesn't matter. You will feel better after that weight is lifted.

I called a meeting with Head Coach David, and he was refreshingly chilled and blasé about it. It was no skin off his nose as he had another new coach and her husband starting next week. I decided to give all my pupils to her and even handed over my coach's diary, so she had all their time slots and numbers she needed. It felt like a nice thing to do and would give her a head start with her client base. I went home that evening feeling such relief.

It had been an intense 11 years on ice and I needed a break. Maybe I'd go back to it, but I knew I needed a lot of time to pass before that happened. I was immensely grateful for everything that sport had given me; what it taught me, where it took me, how it built me, how it broke me, who it made me and everything my mum sacrificed for making my dream a reality. But my 'dream' was no longer serving me, and right now, I had new ones.

Chapter 21 –Changing Direction

While figuring out my next move, I continued with my acting classes and ballet lessons. I kept them going even when I stopped competing. I enjoyed it so much, even though I never had great feet for pointe work, after spending my formative years with my feet encased in what were essentially concrete wellies with blades. But from the waist up, I wasn't half bad! I passed Level 6 with distinction, then just continued for fun and the love of floating my arms around in a leotard.

After the showcase at the acting school, I decided to quit there too. Again, something that NOBODY does. Kate apparently didn't attend her own acting school's showcase, as you would hope. She wasn't lurking in the shadows as I tried to see beyond the burning, bright lights in my eyes while onstage. Oh no, she was in London. I was starting to question if she even existed and the person I met was just a great con woman, and this whole 'acting school' was one big hustle. When I told the lady on reception that I wouldn't be returning next week, she was shocked. She tried to convince me that by leaving I'd have to re-join the waiting list if I wanted to ever come back, and that process could take years. Also, how privileged I was to have bypassed the waiting list in the first place and be granted a place there by Kate herself. I resisted the urge to reply, "Yes, love, but Kate is clearly using me as nothing more than one of her many minions that pays her direct debits and funds her flashy lifestyle and plaques on the wall." I just smiled sweetly instead and slid my parking ticket across the desk for her to validate it for me.

Right then, I asked myself, was there any other pointless shit to eradicate from my life? I was on a roll here. I decided I'd be my own agent and subsequently got myself a lead role in a short film production called Chelsea, playing none other than, Chelsea. It was unpaid, of course, but a great experience and for a great cause. It was to be entered into a competition of short films showcasing diversity. I took to it like a duck to water and was so happy to have a camera shoved in my face again! There was almost zero budget, so I got to style myself and I'd definitely drawn the long straw for once. The poor girl playing opposite me had to accidentally wet herself in the main scene, and I had to save the day by pushing her into a lake to hide the wet patches on her grey jogging bottoms, shoving her in the water and drenching her all over. It was a freezing day and she was indeed a girl, not a stunt guy sporting shadowy facial stubble. The film went on to win the award for the 'best short film' against all the others in the category at the premiere night. It might have been a more modest event than movie premieres you see on TV, but there was a decent amount of people there, and to watch myself extra huge as my already big face lit up the theatre cinema screen, I felt like I'd made it.

"What did you do last night, Soph?"

"Went to my own film premiere, where I collected an award onstage when it was awarded 'best film'..." Definitely beats going to the ice rink or sitting at home watching other girls on TV, in roles that I auditioned for. It was an amazing night. That role was something else really strong to put on my CV, and I didn't even have to wet myself. Things were looking up!

The days began to pass, and I still had a worryingly clear diary and too much time to think. I had some big realisations but there was still a lot I was trying to make sense of and digest.

Sometimes you have to acknowledge your weaknesses and make them into strengths, although they do vary massively from one day to the next in the acting world. It all depends what they're looking for right now. On that day.

For that project. I couldn't seem to catch a break. Having some head space away from the rink and Kate's theatre workshops gave me some much-needed time to step back and look at myself. What have I achieved? What makes me happy now, and where am I going? I realise this is a conversation most 18-year-olds would have with themselves when they're in their mid- to late-20s, but I'd packed in so much already. I probably had the emotional age of a 30 year old. If all the roles available for girls my age I was unsuitable for, or was unwilling to do, maybe now isn't the right time for me to pursue acting? If everyone says what a great personality I've got, why am I trying to be someone else? Maybe I should pursue TV presenting instead? And if I wasn't getting roles because I was "too pretty," maybe I should be trying modelling? It was some seriously stodgy food for thought.

I busied myself with random jobs like babysitting, bar work (where I lasted two weeks), and extra work which just so happened to be at Hollyoaks. Your call time would be 8 a.m., but they wouldn't use you till nearly 6 p.m. It was very interesting but not exactly enjoyable suddenly being at the very bottom of the food chain. Especially after having a taste of what I'd experienced being on Thin Ice. Then, here I was, nothing more than a human prop. We'd sit in the canteen together all day, us fellow extras, eating jacket potatoes and beans, talking about our many other random jobs and big acting dreams. I didn't want to dash their hopes, but you could tell just looking at half of them, they were going to struggle. And the possibility of them putting Leonardo DiCaprio out of a job was highly unlikely. It was a bit like those hopefuls on X Factor waiting for their first audition, having had zero experience but still believing they'll sell out Wembley next month. Good luck to them. I guess anything's possible, but there was more chance of the canteen selling out of beans.

The bar job was never a good idea for a non-drinker with zero knowledge of spirits, wine or the names of any alcoholic beverages. The customer would watch in despair as I'd have to read every bottle label to work out which one was dark rum for their coke, then proceed to put the ice in after I'd poured it, as it spilled over and I handed them a sticky wet glass. Thankfully it was only a posh hotel bar, so never particularly busy on the 6 till 10 p.m. weekday shifts I was working. I only went and got myself a job there because Mum had a vivid dream that 'there was something for me there'...*

*[Read this as 'You'll meet your future husband there and within a few months you'll have a massive rock on your finger! Get in the car and drop them in a copy of your CV NOW!' So, I did. Purely to humour her, but they did indeed have a part-time vacancy.]

During my trial shift with the young, pompous bar manager in his cheap satin waistcoat, the girl who I was replacing came in to say hi and flash her giant engagement ring. It was her who'd met her future husband while serving him on the bar when he was staying there on business. He not long after proposed and she quit her job, and he assured her she'd never have to work another day in her life as he was in fact a millionaire.

Mum's psychic dream was scarily accurate. Apart from the fact it was my former colleague who was off to live the life of luxury, and it was me that was now stuck with a new part-time job I didn't actually want. As I was mostly useless behind the bar but great at pulling a pint, they opted to have me working the floor doing table service. I loved chatting to people, including a con man who stayed there for nearly a week. He had us all fooled with his intricate stories, completely rinsed us, then did a runner, never to be seen again! I quite liked the fact I'd had the excitement of conversing with a professional con man for nearly a week. Although I kicked myself for not sussing him out. I couldn't help but admire his ability for holding his nerve and having an immediate, legit sounding answer for everything. He'd be great being interrogated at a Paris Hilton's New Best Friend audition.

I completed my two week trial shift by mostly asking customers did they want 'red, white or pink' and getting them to open their own wine. I was fine with most screw tops but couldn't pull a cork out even if my life was on the line for it. I would end up accidentally flicking bits of it at the customers till it was almost disintegrated, and they'd eventually say, "Give it here, I'll do it myself."

Dropping my tray was a regular thing, or I'd hold onto it as one beer bottle fell, and I'd watch them all topple over like dominoes. It was a completely mutual decision that I'd be leaving once I'd completed the two weeks.

"You're great at chatting with the customers and making them feel welcome, but I think you'd be better suited to a job on one of those makeup counters," the manager said.

"I absolutely agree!" I beamed. "That's so nice of you to say. I'm actually very good at spraying people and would be great at helping them choose the right shade of lip gloss."

I handed over my apron there and then, and he didn't make me work the rest of my shift. I skipped off home with a smile, feeling like that was the easiest thing I'd ever left – ever! Far less stressful than dumping a dance partner or turning down a contract with a world-class ice show. It worked out perfectly as the dance school where I was doing my ballet classes was putting on their biannual showcase. Seven shows in a week, performing onstage at one of

Manchester's most famous auditoriums. I adored performing onstage each night and got on so well with the other girls. Some nights we'd go out for late night food afterwards, still in our show make up, and laugh at how I nearly took out the cello player when I did my butterfly kick.

I still had a thirst for performing, either in front of a camera or live audience. It burned inside me and still does. After much research, I decided to take myself to London for a TV presenter training course. I figured this would get me back in front of a camera, learning new skills like autocue, and would give me a showreel, all while being completely myself. I loved running around the streets of London with my little camera crew, running up to someone and shoving my microphone in their face. Or recording pieces in the studio and realising the faster you talk, the faster the autocue goes. (Mental note made: slow it down a bit, don't try and catch it up!)

I then threw myself into applying for presenter roles and auditions, all unpaid, as I had no experience but some formal training from the course and a half decent showreel. There was very little being posted on the random castings website I was subscribed to, which is probably why I got booked instantly for my first 'gig'.

It was to compare an event called, 'Search for a West End Star', and was a talent show for 5- to 16-year-olds. It sounded pretty good but turned out to be at an old working men's club in a run-down northern town. It resembled the most grotty ice rink bars, with a low ceiling and sticky patterned carpet. In that sense, I felt quite at home. Apart from feeling like I would get mugged walking to and from my car, or I'd find it burnt out and on bricks at the end of the night.

Some of the kids were hugely talented, while a few were just obnoxious with overinflated egos. Still, I found something positive or diplomatic to say about each one, to ensure their terrifying 'Uncle Dave' (who was probably a gypsy king) didn't kick off at me. I loved being up at the front with my crackly mic and the organiser was so pleased with me that she gave me a tenner towards my petrol. I was made up! We all have to start somewhere, right? Making it home unscathed was an added bonus.

The next audition was for an actual paid role! A whole £50 per recording should I be used on the regular. I'd be embarking into the corporate world to be a pop-up presenter when you'd visit various companies' websites. Imagine me popping up in the bottom left corner of your screen, reciting the painfully boring paragraph about optimising Google so you didn't have to actually read it... Not the most showbiz or relatable market but it would pay. I still got a spray tan done specially and rocked up in my highest heels. It must have been a different type of tan though, because despite rinsing off the excess in the morning, it had left me horrendously shiny! Shiny to the point that the camera operator was complaining of the glare off my face, and a woman from the office started handing me tissues to pat my face because she thought I was sweating excessively. How embarrassing! I explained it was a new spray tan and obviously too oily for my already oily skin. It's probably my own fault for asking to be double dipped. The camera guy and boss man obviously couldn't relate or care less about my skin care problems or erratic T-zone oil production. I still believe it was a bad spray tan that lost me that job. I'd memorised the entire script perfectly so I could eyeball the camera and talk with my hands. Something we'd not been asked to do but I thought it'd make me stand out from everybody else who had their head in their scripts. Or maybe I did just smell really badly of biscuits?

My so-called acting agent did occasionally remember I existed, sporadically sending me for commercial castings for big mobile networks or a famous bread brand. Both of which I got callbacks for and then was shortlisted. The pay would have been phenomenal, and I could have lived off it for ages, affording better spray tans and not dropping trays in a bar. But sadly, no. The life game of Snakes and Ladders continued, and I'd nearly made it once again – even if it was just a short-term version of 'made it'.

I wasn't one to sit around and the year soon passed as I busied myself with acting courses, extra work, babysitting, baking, being my own agent, going to the gym and being there for my family as mum broke her arm in a freak fall, and my beloved Nana passed away a week later. I'll never forget the two huge butterflies trapped in the church during the funeral. They fluttered round, dancing in the air the entire time and I knew it was my Nana and grandad Poppa. Back together again. If there's ever a good way to go, it's the way they did. Living life to the absolute full, right till the end, and even, like Nana, making the best of everything despite her health deteriorating. I've never known anyone to take their medication with champagne, but she did. Swilling down various pills like that on the daily, while dripping in costume jewellery, drenched in Chanel perfume and rocking bright pink and purple nails. I intend to carry on this legacy but swallowing my multivitamins instead.

Chapter 22 – The Golden Triangle

Applying myself and putting myself out there as much as I could was important and time consuming, but it wasn't actually earning me any money. I didn't have many local friends to go out with and sitting in watching TV with my parents every night started to make me feel very unfulfilled! I was desperate to get out there, whatever that entailed, preferably wearing something glamorous. I couldn't see myself being a supermarket checkout girl or wearing a disgusting uniform, but I wanted to be out meeting and talking to people. I wanted something to occupy my evenings and weekends that wasn't Coronation Street, and would leave me free for potential auditions during the day. I'd already ruled out bar work and waitressing as I was awful with a tray, so hot plates were a no-go.

I know what you're thinking: I'm running out of options here... and I was! But after process of elimination and taking into account my 'Will and Won't do's', I decided I'd be great as a hostess at a fancy venue: meeting and greeting, taking bookings and featuring general front-of-house glamour and socialising. I spent all evening updating my CV, printing off numerous copies. I got up the next morning and told Mum and Dad I was going out to find a job and I'd be home when I got one.

I decided to start in my hometown of Altrincham, working my way through to Hale village, Wilmslow and beyond, until I'd dropped my CV in every suitable venue I passed. It was a bit awkward when I'd go into the perfect place yet be greeted by a hostile, overly made-up hostess, basically saying I wanted her job. I'd smile and hand her my CV, knowing she'd probably spit on it and bin it after I leave. But she had probably never read a CV from a former pro ice skater turned TV actress before.

I kept going: pulling over, nipping in each place, ask to speak to the manager, hand over CV, same spiel...until I found myself at the furthest point: Alderley Edge, home to numerous celebrities, footballers and more millionaires per square mile than anywhere else outside of London. It may be the furthest place on my hit list but it was certainly the glitziest and would do nicely. It was only as far as going the other way and ending up in Manchester City centre, and I'd much rather work in the 'Golden Triangle', as it was called, traveling down Cheshire's country lanes instead of battling match day traffic if United were playing at Old Trafford. There was a parking space waiting right outside for me at the biggest and busiest restaurant bar on the High Street: Fino.

As soon as I walked in, I could absolutely see myself working there. With its high ceilings, open theatre kitchen, spiral staircase, front terrace with cute hedges, VIP booths and a bar with a sliding ladder to reach the most expensive bottles, this was definitely my kind of place! I also knew there was only one more place to hit after this before I got to Macclesfield Forest. An efficient Italian waiter went and got the manager from the downstairs office and this painfully thin but friendly lady emerged, dressed head to toe in black, with thick framed glasses poised on her face. We sat down in the bar area, she interviewed me there and then and offered me a job. Wow! That was easy. I was to start in two days' time, which was perfect as tomorrow was my 20th birthday! I immediately spent it shopping for little black dresses and heels for my cool new job. It was the best birthday present ever. A new job, a new wardrobe and a new lifestyle! I was so excited by the thought of being out past 10 p.m. with a purpose other than 'just going for a drive', and not to mention all the new people I would meet.

My first day was a full day shift on a sunny Sunday, shadowing head hostess Amy, who would soon be going on maternity leave. She was so lovely, and I was glad I could pick up her 1 p.m. till 10 p.m. Sunday shift. As it was only minimum wage and no tips, I needed all the hours I could get, but I was so happy to be there earning £5 something an hour and spending it all on blow dries, than I ever was earning £30 plus an hour at the rink.

Amy was great for giving me the lowdown on the locals, the regulars and the many VIPs who would often turn up unannounced and you had to sit them on a booth, whether you had them booked up or not. I watched as all the different cliques drifted in throughout the day. The wealthy families who clearly never cooked at home and their three spoiled kids all under 10, dressed head to toe in Ralph Lauren and would tell you how they like their steak cooked. Child, you're 8! Have some chicken nuggets and be grateful!

There were the millionaires who'd come in with that much younger, blonde second wife. The teenagers and 20 somethings with no jobs but would ride round in Daddy's Lamborghini when he lent them the keys, and their claim to fame was being on an MTV The Hills-style reality show about the area. It only ran for one series. Probably because everyone realised they had zero personalities and it was such a small pond, they'd all slept with one another by episode 3. There were the lonely, single males who'd come in almost every night, alone, for a glass of red, but knew everyone in there so would always end up dining with someone.

Then there were the footballers and drug dealers. Two sets of clientele I knew nothing about but would soon learn maybe too much...

It wasn't long before it hit me how everyone knew everyone's business here. In fact, it was my first day. A local millionaire and regular came in with his much younger second wife. She was Slovakian, tall, blonde, horrendously thin, botoxed, plumped and implanted, deeply tanned and unbelievably glamorous.

"Wow, look at her!" I whispered, somewhat in awe.

"She's bald," quipped Craig, the larger-than-life, loudmouth gay head waiter.

"Bald? She doesn't look it to me, those hair extensions are probably worth £1000 alone!"

"No silly, down there! Her vagina," snapped Craig, crudely, as he turned on his heels and waltzed off to the disabled loo where he appeared to spend a lot of his time... That was information I didn't need to know. Both Craig's toilet habits or this woman's waxing regime. More worryingly, how was this even common knowledge? I shrugged it off and went outside to lay fresh cutlery and linen on one of the patio tables. It was a beautiful, warm afternoon and most people wanted to sit outside. Although it was a small space, it was great for people watching and seeing the chauffeur-driven Rolls Royces pull up. As I laid the table like the most OCD person in the world, a man's voice behind me went "I like your red thong..."

I froze as a million things rushed through my head. Who said that? Did I really just hear that? HOW does he know I'm wearing a red thong? Is my dress tucked into my knickers? No.

"Excuse me?" I said, turning round to find an eerily calm gentlemen, sipping wine on his own with slicked back hair and a creepy icy glare. He looked like a bond villain without a Persian cat on his lap.

"I can see it shining in the light" he replied. Barely moving, barely blinking. "What's your name, you must be new?"

I didn't know what to say, as my cheeks burned with horror and confusion that somehow this random man could see my underwear. I managed a "Yeah, it's my first day. I'm

Sophie. Sorry, I'm needed inside!" as I brushed past him, straight to find Amy. She could tell I was rattled by something and asked what was up. I explained how some random guy outside can somehow see my underwear and commented on it, as I quickly made her inspect the back of my dress for levels of opaqueness.

"Only when the sun hits it and it's really bright. You can just about see a slight glow of red underneath it...but you'd have to look very close and very hard," she reassured me. Great. So my cheap Primark LBD wasn't a problem; it was only the creepy guy outside I had to worry about. She asked who'd said it and I pointed to his greasy slicked back head.

"Oh, that's Will. He's like that." Amy sighed.

Noted. Pervy regular number one. Other than a few awkward or over- familiar interactions, my first day went without a hitch and I loved every minute of strutting around in my high heels and bouncing my blow dry.

The first few weeks were more about learning the locals, VIPs and trying to look busy even if I wasn't. I'd run around collecting dirty glasses and practising with a tray. This was great if I dropped it, as it was just smashed glass I'd have to deal with rather than being drenched too. I also quickly had to get used to the highly sexualised environment. Crude comments, insane flirting and general sleaziness, were standard. The worst for this weren't the openly horny 20-something bartenders or cheating husbands, it was Craig. The loud and proud gay waiter with a mouth like a gutter. He was larger than life and high as a kite most of the time. He would bully me and sexually harass me constantly. Randomly groping my boob as he walked past or lifting up my skirt in front of a packed bar area, exposing my bare bum, then running away cackling loudly, shouting, "Ooh, dirty bitch! Sophie's wearing a thong!"

He was in his 40s but acted like a warped child who'd seen too much at too young an age. His much younger boyfriend Jack, who also worked there, was a total sweetheart. Such a gentle soul. I loved working with him as he'd constantly shake his head and apologise for his boyfriend's outrageously inappropriate behaviour. I couldn't understand why Craig was a law unto himself. Other staff and management were right there when he'd do these things to me but never pulled him up about it. He could tell I was a nice girl and was an easy target to bully or humiliate with disgusting comments.

"How many guys have you slept with?" He'd screech. I'd hesitate, not knowing how to respond. This was very personal information, so I'd usually reply with a, "A lady never tells..." But he wouldn't stop. He'd machine gun me with comments like "Do you like anal? I bet you do, you slut!"

He loved having an audience and would get louder and more creative the more people were there. Like creeping up behind me and putting a massive linen laundry sack over my head. Blinding me and disorientating me, as he picked me up and threw me screaming into the disabled toilets. I emerged, humiliated, fluffing my hair and eyebrows back to normal as all the bar area and diners roared with laughter. This was sexual harassment on the daily, but no one was batting an eyelid. He was very good at his job, wild personality aside. Customers would book in and request to be served by him and would tip him generously without fail every time. He was like the resident entertainer, often breaking into dancing and twirling around the spiral staircase like a stripper. I didn't want to let one idiot spoil my perfect little job that I was enjoying so much. I loved all my other colleagues, even if (looking back) they were only being nice to me so I'd seat more people in their sections and they'd get more tips.

The chefs were complete perverts but full of banter, as they'd send me to the walk-in fridge to look for a 'leg of seabass'. Or the Polish pizza chef who'd ask every day when we were getting married, while staring at me going "Corrr!" and frantically kneading his dough.

I seemed to be an instant hit with the patrons and I was quickly making friends and swapping numbers as they'd invite me to join in on their nights out when I finished my shift. My Facebook friend requests were soaring, which back then was the measure of your popularity. I even traded in my phone early so I could get a white BlackBerry and 'BBM' people, which was all the rage! "What's your BlackBerry pin?" was asked more than "What's your number?' I got clip in hair extensions and started backcombing to resemble Cheryl's hair from girl band Girls Aloud, and very quickly I appeared to be in with the 'in' crowd... Wherever I went round Hale, Wilmslow or Alderley Edge people knew me as 'Fino girl'. The girl who works on the door, takes the bookings, meets and greets, sits you down and makes sure you're always having a wonderful time. Everyone wanted to know me because they thought I could hook them up with a table, even at the busiest times. This wasn't always the case though, as Fino was the busiest restaurant in the village and we were always full. I tried to treat everyone the same, though, as in my eyes, everyone was a VIP.

This theory didn't always go to plan as I once offered a premiership footballer a crappy table in the bar as we were at capacity in the restaurant, and he didn't have a booking. He took it as he was clearly desperate for his pizza and chips. I didn't have a clue who he was until the manager on duty came up from the office, freaking out saying, "Why the hell is

Michael Carter on table 4? He plays for England and should be in a booth!"

"Sorry, I didn't have one available and didn't know who he was." I shrugged.

I was sent home that night being told to read OK! magazine and learn my footballers as my homework. Plus acknowledge the paparazzi who were regularly snooping outside for good reason. "What a great job!" I thought to myself. My homework is to read OK! Magazine! While I skipped back to my car in the dark, this lad got chatting to me.

"You're finished early."

"Not really," I said. "I'm a hostess, not a waitress. I can go when all my bookings are sat."

I recognised him from the day before. He was driving up and down the High Street in an amazing white Lamborghini with a very handsome friend.

"Not riding in your friend's Lambo tonight then?" I asked, realising that probably sounded rather condescending and a hell of a lot more bolshy than I actually was.

"It's technically mine, my mate was just driving it home." (Yeah, right!)

"Good for you! What do you do for a living?" I asked, wondering what lie he'd come out with next. Maybe he'd say "footballer," in which case I'd make a mental note to always seat him in a booth if he ever came into Fino, to avoid getting shouted at by my managers.

"I just chill. My parents are loaded. Add me on Facebook- I'm called 'Curly Wurly'." And with that, he disappeared off down an alleyway with a guy and a girl, to probably do some dodgy dealings.

Wow. Okay, another very Alderley Edge encounter. I still had much to learn: like why so many people said they were businessmen or property developers; why Craig hadn't been sacked 10 times over; and where actually was the lady who interviewed me and gave me the job in the first place?

Chapter 23 - The Honeymoon's Over!

I really was enjoying my new lifestyle of lie-ins, quiet afternoons then glamming up and heading out to work before getting in around midnight. It was like I'd flipped my day around! Not to mention the fact I was finally building a social life and getting attention from guys who didn't have blades on their feet for the first time ever! I couldn't quite believe how I'd landed this fun and relatively easy job. Until I turned up for work one day and it all changed.

I waltzed in wearing my new heels, being greeted by the customers who'd got to know me over the past three weeks, receiving compliments and pecks on the cheek by all the bartenders, as I arrived for the start of my shift.

"Right Sophie, it's me and you tonight!" snapped a stern, female voice.

I turned around. It was Julie, the lady who'd interviewed me but I'd never seen since. Turns out she'd been on holiday the past few weeks and she was in fact the general manager and resident jealous Uber Bitch, who set out to make my life hell and treat me like Cinderella. She immediately sent me to the toilets to inspect them, tidy round and replenish loo roll. This included the men's, where I had to knock and shout, "Excuse me, is there anyone in there?" and a gruff voice said "Yeah babe, come in!" Eeww. Then it was onto cleaning windows and outside to sweep up cigarette butts. She stood there watching me, arms folded and an evil smirk on her face like she was Maleficent. An older gentleman smoking a cigar outside piped up, "You're far too glamorous to be doing that! Give it here," as he grabbed the dustpan and brush and started doing it for me, much to Julie's annoyance. Maybe she was in a bad mood because she was suffering holiday blues?

"Sit this next booking on table 30. Go on! Go! MOVE!" she snapped, physically prodding me and pushing me away with the menus. When I returned, she handed me a cloth and spray, telling me to get cleaning the heavily soiled high chairs which were covered in crusty pasta sauce and actual baby sick.

It was the shift from hell and I couldn't work out what her problem was with me. Maybe I could use this time to talk to her about the way Craig behaves and how inappropriate it is? It turned out to fall on deaf ears, as those two were thick as thieves. Laughing and joking together, and I watched as she let him take countless cigarette breaks, yet I wasn't even allowed to reapply my lip gloss. She responded with an "Oh Sophie! It's all in good humour! You'll have to grow a thicker skin if you're working in this industry."

It was like being told to 'shut up and put up' with Daniel's behaviour all over again.

"Anyway, you've done well tonight," she quipped. Sounding every inch the Jekyll and Hyde, signing 11pm on my hours card, even though it was 11:20.

"See you Friday!" she smirked.

What a bitch! The honeymoon was well and truly over, and I began to live for the shifts when I was rota'd on without her. Maybe I could just spend the other shifts running away from her and hiding behind the pillars? Or changing the ashtrays outside and taking an abnormally long time to do so.

Unfortunately, things were about to get much worse...

Fino was launching a home delivery service: restaurant food delivered to your door. At the time, this hadn't really been done before and had apparently been months in the making.

Interesting. Not my department though as I was a Hostess, right? Wrong!

As I trotted into work holding my brand-new, purple platform heels to change into, Julie greeted me by saying, "You won't be needing those tonight, I've got a special job for you..." while she creepily put her arm around me, leading me to the kitchen. Tonight, I would be cutting pizzas, boxing them up and filling up sauce pots for the deliveries. Are you kidding me? This made the Polish pizza maker's day, and I suppose I did make friends while folding boxes with the delivery driver. We stood there waiting for the phone to ring, in what was basically a very hot cupboard just off the kitchen. Frustratingly, you could still hear all the people out in the front enjoying themselves. I longed to be back out there, front of house. So many of my new friends came in that night and thought I wasn't in. No, I was just in a box around the back!

Half my shifts became takeaway shifts on the phones. But they did hold their own little burst of excitement when you realised you were talking to a celebrity or the most famous WAG of all, and they were literally telling you their phone numbers and where they lived. Not to mention their clear love for mushrooms as they ordered extra extras on their pizza. While most people would order a two-litre bottle of Pepsi to wash it all down with, they'd order a bottle of Dom Perignon or Crystal, and maybe a lime for the husband's beer. Fascinating stuff! – as was Google imaging their addresses to drool over the size of their electric gates.

It would rarely go smoothly though, as there was often only one driver and if you had a flurry of orders or said driver got stuck, we'd have to improvise. That meant me delivering the pizzas myself. The only problem was I'd be dressed in my usual glam hostess attire, as often I had to float between the two: boxing pizzas one minute, sitting down VIPs the next. I was more than happy to drive to some of these fancy houses, but I guess it did look slightly bad when a footballer opens the door and I'm stood there in my heels, fishnets and leopard-print trench coat, holding a margarita. Was this an additional, special service being put on by Fino for their elite clientele, supplying a pizza hooker? (I'd forgive you for thinking that.) Thankfully, no. This was just me, mucking in because the actual delivery driver got stuck behind Wayne Rooney's electric gates, so they sent me instead.

Despite these players being on over 150 grand a week, one of them had a serious problem with the £2.50 delivery charge, and was always kicking off to me on the phones while ordering his lasagne. Sometimes the takeaway shifts would be a God send as I'd have a definite 11pm finish. Perfect for heading out afterwards to one of the three other bars in the village and meeting up with all the people I'd just seen in the restaurant. Everyone would start at the top of the High Street and work their way down, all ending up in Elixir Bar & Club till the small hours. These champagne-fuelled, 'it crowd' types were rarely ready to go home at 2am, so there'd often be an afterparty going on at one of the huge houses or penthouses close by.

I remember one baby-faced 18-year-old inviting us all back to a wing of his parent's house, and when we got there it had a moat around it. These people clearly had no need for an overdraft! People hardly slept in this village. Customers or colleagues. Despite their often unhealthy lifestyles, they were all skinny with endless energy. You're probably thinking I'm being horrendously naive, and you'd be right. The following day the biggest penny dropped right on my head...

A Sunday day shift with the usually hyper Craig, who was uncharacteristically down. Depressed almost. Telling us all to "Fuck off" out of his way for merely walking past him. Until a boy racer looking car pulled up outside... Craig ran out, reached in through the window, taking his tip money out of his back pocket and replacing it with a scrunched-up packet of something. He then ran inside to the toilets and emerged less than 10 minutes later, higher than the highest kite. He went round nearly all the staff, subtly high fiving them, dispensing portions to each one of them, before heading down to the office with a very giddy looking Julie. It all made sense now! Craig could do whatever the hell he wanted and was utterly flameproof, as he was supplying the staff and (most importantly) the management, with cocaine.

I quickly became hyper-aware of what was going on and just how many people were on this stuff. Most of them clearly couldn't get through a day without it. No wonder the bright orange, muscly guy, on steroids up to his eyeballs, who went by the name of "Hush" was always in here looking so happy. He obviously kept his stash under that weird flat cap he always wore. Not just to conceal his receding hairline through years of taking growth hormone.

Chapter 24 – In with the In Crowd

Sometimes all it takes is one person who has the hook-up to everything, who takes you under their wing and suddenly you find yourself mixing in whole new circles. For me, this was an uber-sociable and delightfully friendly guy called Nathan. I got chatting to him walking back to my car one night, as he and his best mate had come out of Fino's very tipsy and were fumbling to light one another's cigarettes. They'd been in the restaurant all evening and were some of the nicer more down-to-earth regulars. Nathan was a laugh-a-minute kind of person and he immediately treated me like a long-lost little sister, putting his arm around me and promising to introduce me to all the best people and places, along with protecting me from the many snakes and general gangsters in the village.

"We only hang with good people, Soph! I want you to meet all our friends! They'll love you. You're one of us, I can tell! Why don't you come out with us on Saturday? It's my cousin's birthday party and her best mate is in town," he chatted on. I got a good vibe from him straight away, and his easy-going style and nature was a refreshing antidote from the customer who just told me to be careful hanging his coat up, as it was 'custom made for £3,500'.

"That's nice! Mine's twenty quid from Primark," I replied, draping his old-man-style tweed jacket over my arm and quickly moving out of his obnoxious aura.

Saturday night came and I whizzed through my hostess shift, buzzing off the weekend atmosphere and the fact I had an actual party to go to afterwards. I finished at 11:30 but Julie signed me out at 11pm (typical), and I jumped in my little pinked-up car, changed my heels into even higher ones and drove through to the neighbouring village of Wilmslow. When I parked outside Rebellion Bar, the queue was down the street. My heart sank a bit as I wasn't convinced I'd make it in. I BBM'd Nathan and moments later he appeared at my car to escort me in and handed me a VIP wristband.

"Here, put this on," he said.

We sashayed past the queue of people, through the group of doormen, free of charge and straight up to our own area in VIP. His birthday girl cousin wasn't actually there yet and when I asked where she was, he assured me she was on her way, but her celebrity best mate was joining her, so things were taking a little longer as they tried to avoid paparazzi and getting mobbed by fans. Naturally, I asked who it was and even my completely sober self nearly toppled over when he told me: A member of the biggest girl band of the moment – who was constantly in the tabloids for her rock 'n roll ways – was about to rock up any second, and it just so happened Nathan's cousin went to school with her, and they go way back! I couldn't quite believe it, but this was 'The Golden Triangle of Cheshire' after all, so nothing should surprise me. I saw some commotion on the dance floor below and people screaming but no popstar insight. Maybe it was just a girl's hair catching fire from the sparklers in the bottles of vodka. Whether she turned up or not, I didn't mind. I was living my best life, dancing away in my new shoes, with my new friends and a whole pitcher of pineapple juice all to myself.

"Ok, she's in the building!" Nathan shouted down my ear, mid dance-move.

"Are you serious?!" I had my momentary doubts but sure enough, there she was, staggering out of the toilets, completely off her face, escorted by two much more sober friends. Within minutes she was draped all over me, sloshing her drink everywhere, breathing in my face, telling me

EVERYTHING! About anything. Literally right up close till I went cross-eyed. I pulled away, desperately trying to refocus my vision, trying to see if what was happening was even real. It was, and she was all over me like a long-lost best friend. Two hours ago I was taking restaurant bookings and running round collecting dirty glasses, trying to avoid Julie. Fast forward to now, and I'm partying with one fifth of the biggest girl band in years! Or should I say babysitting her? It did worry me how she couldn't look after herself and was scarily loose-lipped after a few drinks, spilling the beans about her drug habits, rehab and all her celebrity friend's business. Thank God she was saying this to me and not a random, untrustworthy individual who could have so easily recorded this and sold the story to the newspapers.

I, on the other hand, was quite happy and used to shepherding vulnerable drunk people through their nights out, only for it to be documented in my diary the next day. We'd not been out for long but she was so far gone already. I could see the worry spreading across the others' faces as to how the hell they were going to get her out of here without her getting mobbed, falling over, and the hordes of paparazzi out front ready to capture every unflattering moment of it. We needed to leave now, before the lights came on or before she ran out of vodka and started kicking off. We couldn't all fit in a taxi and a taxi would be too obvious. We didn't have far to go – only to Nathan's house for pizza and an after party.

"Guys! I've got a Ford KA so I can fit four passengers if that helps?" I offered.

They all conferred once more. It was blowing my mind they would actually consider putting a huge celebrity in the back of my mum's old car, but it would act as a great decoy!

"Right Soph, this now all revolves around you," Nathan said calmly, as he began to run me through the escape plan of action. I was happy to be of service! When they said the word, I went to get my car, escorted by one of the security staff who directed me round the back, where I parked up at the bottom of the fire escape staircase. The amount of people and paps waiting at the front was insane! It was difficult for even a normal person to push through that wall of people and cameras. The security guard headed up the rickety steps to let them know I was ready. I sat there in the dark, breathing in the fresh night air, listening to the hum of music from inside and wondering if we'd actually pull this off. I was appreciating a moment's peace, only to be disturbed by the ringing of my own ears. Part of me wished the press would catch on and head round to the back of the building, capturing her getting in my pinked-up Ford KA! What a scoop that would be! I could see it now: 'Girl band member escapes in pink Ford decoy car, driven by glamorous sober friend with great shoes!'

I was snapped out of this fun daydream by the fire escape door bursting open, and there she was. Nathan and his cousin had linked her arms either side, one person walking behind and another guy in front, ready to catch her if she toppled forward, as they talked her through how to tentatively put one foot in front of the other.

"This isn't the Merc!" She screamed.

"Shh!" they all hissed, as they eventually got her to ground level and began piling into my car. We decided to put her in the back behind me as it would be more discreet. Although, five people rammed into a four-seater brothel on wheels was hardly discreet, the fluffy 'Princess on Board' sign would shield her face. Unless she ripped it off and lobbed it out of the window.

That plan worked! We took off down the back alley and out onto the connecting main road and no one saw or suspected a thing. We did it! And I must admit, the feeling of foiling the paparazzi and driving the getaway car was the biggest buzz EVER!

It ended up being a much longer drive than I anticipated, though. I had to drive around 30 minutes away to a large house she'd been staying at and had left her phone there. She'd been freaking out all night about it, screaming, "Someone could be ringing Cara!" (fellow bandmate and the nation's favourite.) Or the famous glamour model friend she was often pictured with. I couldn't help thinking her phone being out of her drunken hand and locked in an empty house was by far the best place for it at this time.

I can honestly say she was the worst passenger ever. Pulling on the back of my seat, putting her head on my shoulder shouting, "I love you!", then stupidly trying to put her hands over my eyes as I sped down the winding country lanes. I leant forward over the wheel, amazed that no one else was telling her to stop it. They clearly were used to letting her run wild or never speaking up to her. Like 'don't upset the celebrity!' She slumped back into her seat finally, but then started screaming, "I want my drugs! Get me some now!"

The novelty of having a huge celebrity pop star in my car was quickly wearing off. It was more like having a child screaming for their dummy as she kicked the back of my seat.

Phone retrieved, from whoever's huge, random house it was, we headed back to Nathan's to continue the night. The others from the bar had already got there and had already drank through all the alcohol. As everyone piled out and my pop star liability-of-a-passenger eventually decided which side she wanted to get out of, Nathan and I jumped back in to drive around the corner to the wine bar and get more supplies. He could have easily walked on his own, but I realised he wanted to get me on my own and have a private word with me about what was about to go down...

"What happens in those four walls, stays in those four walls." He said, sternly.

"Of course. I'm not gonna sell a story or post loads of stuff on Facebook. I deal with celebrity types all the time at work." I reassured him.

"I know, but they'll be up to loads of crazy stuff in there." He warned as we parked up on his drive again.

I'm glad he subtly warned me, so it wasn't such a shock when I walked into the kitchen and there was cocaine over all the work surfaces, on the glass coffee table and some random fat guy who'd appeared out of nowhere, completely coked up. I'd never actually seen it in real life but it did look a lot like baking powder. I quickly made my way to the living room where there was just residue of the drug, rather than the snowstorm happening in the kitchen. I wasn't going to stay long with all this going on, although no one pressured me or made me feel uncomfortable for not doing it. Nathan began to frantically reassure me that he himself didn't partake in this and was in fact much like me, as he barely drank now either. I didn't quite believe him, but I gave him the benefit of the doubt.

I sat myself down on the sofa and my pop star new best friend plonked herself next to me.

"So... do you party?" She slurred.

"Errm, not really... I like to dance though!"

"So how did you get involved with Nath then?" she asked, at which point a plate of cocaine and a credit card got passed in front of me. I began to explain how I knew our mutual friend, not that she heard me. The lads suddenly started blasting Bon Jovi and Bryan Adams hits, and we both simultaneously jumped up and started dancing. She demanded I try on her Christian Louboutins as they were 'magic dancing shoes'. I gladly obliged. I'd always dreamt of owning my own pair one day and I guess trying hers on was a good omen. An hour of dancing in her shoes passed, and I went to the kitchen to get some water. Nathan's friend Ben put his arm around me.

"How are you doing Soph? Glad you could join us tonight."

"Yeah, thanks for inviting me! It's been...fun! If a little surreal." I replied, as PC as possible. But when I looked up, I noticed he was having a nose bleed! This was too much now. I felt utterly disgusted and horrified in equal measures. It was time for me to make a quick exit. I said my goodbyes and tried to hide my disgust in Ben and everyone's recreational drug habits.

What an interesting night. And an eye opening one at that. I eventually crawled into bed at 4:50am, thinking how I'd be writing this night up in my diary for weeks! The next morning, I was up at 9am to get ready for work and began to question whether everything that happened last night was just a very farfetched dream. But no! When I went out to inspect the damage to the car's inside, I was pleased (and somewhat relieved) to find the only thing my pop star friend had left behind was her Chanel eyeliner. A welcome souvenir from the night, which I gave to my mum as it was her colour.

While I reflected on the night and people's behaviour, it hit me how sad it was that many couldn't have a decent night without shovelling a load of class A's up their nose. They weren't bad people. The bad people were the drug dealers who take advantage of their weaknesses or unhealthy choices. I felt safe and secure in myself and my morals, knowing I'd never have the desire to ingest anything so pointless and potentially deadly, that had more than likely been up someone's bum to get in the country. No thanks! Give me a picture of pineapple juice and Michael Jackson's 'PYT' on repeat and the night is mine.

Chapter 25 – Ballers and Friends

I guess if you have more money than you know what to do with, aside from spending it on pointless or illegal things, you may also want to help your friends out so they too can share in your glamorous lifestyle and be free from financial strains. I noticed this happening a lot amongst the footballers, particularly. They'd all have that one friend who would go everywhere with them and do everything for them, however big or small. They'd sport the same designer tracksuits, flashy Rolexes and a string of desperate wannabe WAG girls following them. Even though they themselves weren't actually a footballer. They were the wingmen. I couldn't quite imagine paying my best friend to be my friend, but if it meant they could hang out with me all the time in my millionaire bubble and not have to work a normal job, I'm sure I'd do it too. The most popular pair on the scene were Dwayne and Kane. They ate at Fino almost every day and had been best mates since primary school. A true double act, with their cheeky cockney humour, strong jaw lines, cheesy grins and constant banter. They were definitely the most likeable of the footballer-wingman duos! Almost every night, I'd turn up for work and the top booking would be for 'Kwayne' – the Brangelina bromance of Alderley Edge.

Despite Kane's rise to fame as a premiership footballer and his high profile, he actually seemed quite shy. Larger than life Dwayne would do most of the talking for him, while he'd gaze at me with his piercing blue eyes. As far as I knew, Kane was single as I'd never seen him with a girl before, or heard him speak of one. So, when he asked for my number, I didn't see anything wrong with that. He was painfully shy while asking me, unable to hold his usual icy blue eye contact and I melted a bit.

"Thank God for that! He's been trying to pluck up the courage to ask for your number for ages," shouted Dwayne, pulling him into a brotherly love style headlock as he blushed a rosy red.

This meant rather than asking, "Is Sophie in tonight?" or "What time does she start?" whenever they came in to dine, Kane started texting me, asking for himself. I couldn't believe I had a footballer texting me! Especially one from my grandfather's all-time favourite team. He was a lot more confident on texts than in person, often texting me flirty or complimentary messages while I was working. He'd be sat in a booth with his mates, watching me seating other guests, calling me over every five minutes. Even when they didn't really want anything. I just thought they were impressed with my tray skills, which by now were pretty impressive! Even more so while walking in stilettos at speed. Imagine if condescending Jake from the hotel job could see me now!

I was never quite sure how to respond to the messages. I was rubbish at sending flirty texts and it wasn't really my style. I was waiting and hoping he'd just asked me out for a date, rather than the shy, coy moments where him and Dwayne would simply watch me doing my job, while making small talk with me...like, "What time you working till babe?" Then texting me telling me how nice I looked once they'd left. This was all lovely but frustratingly went on for weeks, and I began to question if he had a wife and kids at home.

I wasn't entirely surprised but I was a bit gutted when he turned up for dinner at Fino with a random 5-year-old that turned out to be his. I really didn't want to date a guy with a kid. I was only 20 and taking on the stepmom role was definitely not what I was looking for. I assumed the kid lived with the mum, and she and Kane were obviously no longer together. There was still a lot of mystery surrounding him, so maybe I was stupid not to go round to his on the numerous times he asked. It could have answered a lot of questions! But I was old fashioned. I never make the first move and was holding out hope of him taking me out.

When he came in to collect over £80 worth of take-out food, he explained he was having a few people over and I should join when I finished my shift. In hindsight, I probably should have, but by the time I had clocked off, it was so late. I knew all the food would have long gone and potentially so would the other guests... A very different dynamic. I texted him to explain my absence: Tired/late, and resisted the urge to say I was starving and knew I had some left-over dinner waiting for me at home. I also didn't want him seeing my badly fake tanned feet when I finally kicked my heels off after a long shift. He replied with a sad face and an "OK, I'll catch you tomorrow xx".

At this rate it would be years before he eventually asked me out! That's where my new, gobby friend came in...

Chloe was an air hostess, a friend of Nathan's, and was casually dating his best mate, 'Pilot Dave', who was an actual pilot and regularly supplied his friends with duty-free cigarettes and booze. He was also casually dating most of his other cabin crew when it was convenient for him. I really liked Chloe and Dave and thought they were a great couple. Always dancing and in high spirits, they constantly looked out for me as if I was a little sister. I liked hanging out with people older than me. They always said what was on their mind. Whether that came with confidence or age or excess alcohol, I wasn't sure, but still. When Chloe marched up to Kane to have a word with him about me, I wasn't going to stop her.

It was a typical busy and glamorous Saturday night in Alderley Edge, and the whole village had worked their way down the High Street after starting in Fino, winding up in the uber exclusive Elixir Bar & Club. It was owned and run by a once notorious gangster who was now a reformed character after getting out of prison. Every weekend the VIP booths would be filled with footballers and the most exclusive bottles of champagne and vodka, displayed in a sunken bed of crushed ice in the centre of their tables. I often found myself on the neighbouring booth as, lucky for me, my friends would often have one booked. This meant I had somewhere to sit, somewhere to dance and somewhere to put my bag, all while helping myself to the free fruit juice mixers.

Chloe and I looked like sisters and she was my dancing partner in crime as well as matchmaker.

"That footballer can't take his eyes off you!" she winked, as we threw shapes to Beyoncé. I looked over to find that Kane, Dwayne and all their mates, were in fact our booth neighbours.

"He's been watching you all night!" Chloe slurred.

"Yeah, I know him," I said, shouting down her ear over the music. I hated it when people did that to me but sometimes it was necessary. "I do like him...," I continued. "We text but he's never asked me out. I think he's lost interest."

Before even replying, she swigged the last of her vodka, marched over to him, vigorously tapping him on his shoulder and yelled "What do you think of that girl over there?!" right in his face. They both turned to look at me, Chloe pointing with her Prada clutch.

"She's not interested in me," he sighed.

"I can tell you she is!" Chloe declared. His eyes widened as he sipped his drink.

"Well then, she'd really like my answer," he said smoothly.

Chloe ran back round to our booth, physically bursting with excitement as she relayed all this to me. Before we had a chance to fully debrief, Kane broke away from his friends and sauntered over to me.

"When can I take you out?" he whispered.

"Whenever you like!" I beamed, having lost all ability to play it cool. "But it depends, are you allowed?" By this I meant was he married, engaged, or involved with anyone else.

"Of course, I'm allowed!" he laughed. Without further questioning, I immediately took his word for it and saw this as a green light. I was eternally grateful to Chloe for being the best big-sister-style friend. And grateful for life in general that, in six months, my Saturday nights had gone from scrolling past reruns of Gardeners' World, at home alone, to being chatted up by a premiership footballer, drinking the finest pineapple juice in a VIP booth with a whole new crowd.

By this point I was gradually getting more savvy and had done a fair bit of Googling. Something I maybe should have done sooner, but back then it felt so weird and unnatural to Google a guy you want to date. (How times have changed.) Shouldn't you get to know them for who they are now, rather than the person they were on Google four years ago? Instead of being bombarded by the old web pages that pop up with highly out of date or inaccurate information? Besides, you shouldn't believe everything you read online. It made me feel a little uncomfortable when it dragged up articles of Kane and his then-fiance and mother of his kid, from his years playing for a top London club. I was knee-deep in page five of stalking Google's search results on him, yet I couldn't find anything recent of him and a girl being linked in any way. Just lots of paparazzi pictures of him coming out of Fino with Dwayne, or the lads' nights out leaving Elixir in the small hours. Everyone has a past, right? It would have been weird had he not had a long-term girlfriend.

I saw him on most of my shifts that week and the flirty messages continued, but still no actual date for dinner or a movie arranged. It was only ever a "Come over to mine babe and we'll watch a movie and chill." A proposition later translated to 'Netflix and Chill' in recent years.

While on a usually boring takeaway shift, waiting for the phone to ring, batting off the Polish pizza chef's perverted (but still flattering) comments, things got a bit more exciting...

Our one delivery driver got stuck in roadworks and the next order was sat there ready to go and getting cold. Great! This usually means I'll get to take it and scive off for half an hour, driving the long way through the country lanes and maybe drive up another very posh driveway. My favourite and non-sexually harassing manager on duty, Tom, flew round to my little cupboard of a nerve centre and frantically checked the wait times on all the tickets with his overly chewed biro.

"Why are all these orders backing up?" he panicked. "And how long's that one been sat there getting cold?!"

I personally couldn't care less as, in my eyes, I wasn't even meant to be round here. I should be out front doing a hostess shift as originally planned.

"Sophie, would you mind delivering this? It's for Dwayne and Kane. He loves you so if you take it, it'll soften the blow that it's late."

"How do you know it's theirs? I asked, wondering how I'd missed this vital piece of info!

"Online order, and that's their usual address. We've delivered to it a thousand times, it's literally five minutes away – just go!" he begged, looking way more stressed than necessary as he stacked up the heat insulated pizza bags in my arms and shuffled me out the door.

Well, this'll be a nice surprise... for both Kane and me! I get to see where he lives but can't stay as I'm technically on shift, and he gets his pizza delivered by his crush. Happy days!

It was literally a three-minute drive and I probably could have walked, just not in these heels, carrying a load of pizzas. Sure enough, the house was stunning. A country manor style residence with a sweeping driveway, complete with two Mercedes and a Porsche to choose from. Dwayne opened the door and he was thrilled to see me as he cheered and threw his arms around me, giving me the biggest hug.

"No way they sent you round! This is mint! Come in, Kane's in the kitchen."

I loved Dwayne. His larger-than-life personality and clear joy to be living the footballer life without even having to kick a ball. There's no way I was going to decline the chance to walk into Kane's amazing kitchen and place their food on no doubt a massive marble island workshop, all while having a damn good nosey.

"Oi, mate! Guess who's delivered our pizza!" Dwayne shouted, as I walked through the stunning hallway into a kitchen fresh out of a posh interiors magazine.

"Surprise!" I smiled, as I emerged through the archway, finding Kane looking down on his phone, perched on one of the stylish breakfast bar stools.

"No way," he mumbled, as he looked up, completely shocked. I immediately sensed his hostility and couldn't understand why he looked far from happy to see me. Especially as the day before he'd been asking about my fishnets and that I should "come over." Fast forward 24 hours and he's looking utterly terrified that I'm finally in his kitchen. I went to greet him with our usual peck on the cheek and he visibly flinched. Do I smell? Was he embarrassed not to be in his usual Hugo Boss tracksuit?

"Sorry about the delay. The driver got stuck so they sent me instead," I continued.

"Yeah, yeah!" laughed Dwayne, "Everyone knows he'd love Sophie on a pizza, who wouldn't?!"

I blushed as a wave of shyness came over me and I giggled. But Kane wasn't laughing. It felt awkward and it was definitely my time to leave. I went to hug him goodbye, but he pulled away, keeping his eyes down, avoiding all contact. This had never happened before! Was I missing something here? Dwayne hugged me goodbye, walking me out and giving me a £10 tip. When I got back in my car, shoving the tip in my bra, I couldn't get away quick enough. My skin was crawling with the awkwardness I had just experienced, my heart felt heavy, head confused.

Once back at the restaurant, the driver had returned and normal service had resumed. Normal in that we'd messed up again. In Tom's hastiness he'd forgotten to put the ice cream in the cooler bag for Kane's order.

"Do you wanna run back with this?" said driver Ryan, waving a tub of cookie dough flavour at me. "I bet he was pleased to see you!" He winked.

"Not really... Dwayne was, but Kane seemed really cold and distant. You go and take it instead." I sighed.

There's no way I wanted to be brushed off again like that. Not today anyway. I couldn't get my head around it and couldn't wait for Ryan to return and see what he thought of Kane's vibe or how he was treated. Sure enough, Ryan arrived back in under 15 minutes with his empty cool bag.

"So, how was he? Sheepish, quiet and awkward with you too?" I asked in hope.

"I dunno, I didn't see him. Some Brazilian woman with black hair opened the door..."

My blood ran cold.

"That's her! That's his fiancé! So she was there the whole time? No wonder he was sheepish when I turned up, if his flippin' fiancé was upstairs!" I seethed.

"Yeah, looks like!" Ryan shrugged. "It looks like she's staying there. She was in her dressing gown and slippers with kind of wet hair. Lousy tipper!"

I shook my head. That whole situation could have been even worse if I was a different sort of girl. I could've really landed him in it. I'm sure most girls would have, then sold their story. And he'd deserve it! WHAT A RAT. All the happy daydreams and scenarios I'd play through in my head got blown to smithereens. Of course, I'd allowed myself to imagine what it might be like dating him: leaving Fino's, then turning up with him a week later on a busy Saturday, having made no booking and watching Julie freak out as she had to give us a booth and mess up her perfect seating plan. But alas, I would've been nothing but his bit on the side, only to be tossed away the moment his Brazilian model fiancé was up visiting from London, trying to piece their relationship back together. I Googled him again the next morning and sure enough that's exactly what happened. According to the Sunday papers, she was tired of his partying ways and had come over to give their relationship one last shot and be a family with their five-year-old son together. How ironic as later that night I saw him and his boys in Elixir bar, apparently having a 'low key' night. Kane ignored me but, in a way, I was ignoring him too. I had nothing to say other than "good luck" to his fiancé. I'd had my first brush with a footballer and their tangled web of a world, and it didn't make me feel particularly good or flattered. How many girls was he doing this to? How many would be happy with being the girl on the side? Probably quite a lot. Especially as all the eligible girls in this affluent village would flock to wherever the players were dining or hanging out with their teammates. Even if they were famously married or much older, it didn't stop them. It was like they had a built-in wannabe WAG radar and would swarm like bees around a honey pot; wearing the most makeup they could fit on their faces, positioning themselves and their friends at the nearest table. Some of them were scarily younger and might as well have handed over their hearts on a plate and said, "There you go, feel free to smash this on the floor!" There was bound to be many girls who were casualties of this.

I was holding out hope that the nice football players were out there. The ones that ended up happily married with kids, and you never hear of any sordid tabloid stories or flirtations with restaurant hostesses. Those footballers had to exist!

Ever the optimist that I was and working in Alderley Edge, you were only ever a couple of shifts away from meeting your next one...

Chapter 26 – Nice to Meet You

Karma's a Bitch and if you're lucky, she'll let you watch. For
me, my kick-ass guardian angel Nana had a helping hand in
this. I was convinced! Shortly after discovering Kane was just
as bad as the rest of them and I was very nearly lined up to
be his next 'bit on the side', he suffered a terrible injury
during a hugely important game with his former team. A bad
tackle resulted in him being stretchered off in agony with
severed tendons in his knee, putting him out of play for
weeks and on a pair of crutches instead. I couldn't help but
think karma was alive and well, as he'd hobble into Fino's
and have to use the disabled loo. I probably should've helped
hold the door open as it was right next to the hostess stand,
but I just smiled and pretended I was on the phone.

Life went on at the restaurant and I continued to
enjoy my little job in this glamorous bubble, serving the
elites of Cheshire, busying myself collecting dirty glasses so I
could stay longer, even once all my bookings had come in.
Showcasing my now brilliant tray skills, putting up with
Craig's gross comments, avoiding psycho boss Julie, batting
off any weirdos and perfecting my ability to suss out a drug
dealer, credit card millionaire or footballer from a mile off!
Well, almost.

One evening I arrived at work to find Julie in the biggest flap
ever. The owner and founder of all the Fino restaurants was
booked in for dinner with his wife, alongside another VIP
booking of a premiership footballer and all his friends. I
didn't see the big deal. This is what we do! Treat everyone the
same and give everyone a great experience. But Julie's
inability to cope with any additional pressure made me
wonder how the hell she ever got the job as manager. I led
everyone to their tables including boss man, telling him what

the specials were and pointing out the cocktail list and toilets, as if he didn't know. His booth neighbours on the table next door were the footballers and a very baby-faced looking friend. I'd not seen him before and he looked like a fish out of water. Probably being trialled as the new wingman or salaried friend. Young and impressionable.

As the evening went on, they were joined by more footballer friends, multiplying in numbers, pulling up chairs, ordering more pizzas and steaks, until half the squad were crammed into the booth! Full of the usual cocky banter, they were calling me over every five minutes and invited me out to join them afterwards at Rebellion Bar, where they had a table in VIP. I said I'd think about it. Knowing full well it would be a cattle market of wannabe WAGs vying for their attention and their bottles of crystal. And I knew myself well enough that, on a weeknight, I would much rather head home after a hectic shift to eat, put my slippers on and watch crap TV.

Boss-man almost outstayed the footballers as he sat there observing long after his meal, relishing the fact these young sportsmen were spending a fortune and lining his pockets. The young baby faced one was just on diet cokes, though, and would almost whisper his order to me as if he was shy of his friends hearing his drink choices. He had a strong north-easterly accent and seemed a little overwhelmed with it all. They eventually piled out onto the pavement, much to the delight of the paparazzi, demanding I come and join them when I finish. Myself, along with 100 other girls I'm sure!

"Enjoy your evening guys, I might join you later. Do you need any taxis ordering?" I asked to the ringleader, somewhat relieved that they were leaving.

"Nah babe, we're good! Just come and join us later, yeah? My mate likes you!"

Yeah right! I thought. I didn't trust that gobby one as far as I could throw him, and I was only small so couldn't throw him very far.

It's always amusing watching a group of highly tipsy people trying to delegate and organise how to all get from one bar to the next. Especially when they could probably walk. Julie made sure to put a stop to any potential after work fun by making me wipe down all 200 menus, just in case I was hoping to get out early. When I looked up mid wipe, my shy Diet- Coke-drinking Geordie friend stood there with his hands in his pockets, waiting to talk to me. Was he lost? Had he forgotten something? No, he politely asked for the number of a local taxi firm.

"Have you spoken to any of those outside?" I asked, pointing to the line of available taxis.

"Erm, no," he replied, sheepishly. This all seemed a bit odd, so I smiled and handed him a card for the local taxi company.

"Here you go! These guys are great."

"Is your number on here? Because that's the one I really want...," he grinned, like he'd just got an injection of confidence from the chat-up line gods.

"Very smooth!" I joked. "I'm not meant to give it out at work, but I might come to Rebellion Bar later."

"I've just moved here and don't really know anyone yet. I'm not a massive drinker, so I don't think I'll be out late. Is it okay if I text you? I'd really like that," he continued. It was the most I'd heard him say all night and I don't know if it was his shyness, awkwardness, soft Geordie tones or the fact he wasn't a massive party animal, but he won me over. There was no written rule to say I couldn't give my number out at work; it just didn't seem very professional. But with waiter Craig and his massive gob away from the restaurant floor, smoking in an alleyway by the bins, and Julie down in the office, the coast was technically clear.

"I'll text you later. We should definitely hang out," he smiled coyly, as he headed out to his impatient friends, beckoning him into a Mercedes. I didn't hold my breath, but I was intrigued by him. Someone clearly a similar age to me and a non-drinker, who's not yet caught up in the Golden Triangle of Cheshire scene. He was quite appealing.

I ended up not going to join them afterwards. Instead, I opted to join my actual friends at a nearby bar after they too had finished a busy restaurant shift. I'd put my new friend Josh out of my head, but true to his word I received a text from him at 2:00 a.m.

"Hey pretty girl. Thanks for your number. We should go out for food next week x"

And so, it begins...

The next morning I was chatting away to Mum and my phone was pinging constantly with messages from Josh. Telling me about his night, how he went home early as the others got too drunk and he was tired, but would have stayed out later if I'd had been there... Considering he comes across so shy, he was definitely a smooth talker and I was keen to learn more about him.

"Your phone's busy this morning!" exclaimed Mum.

"Yeah, it's this guy who asked for my number last night, Josh Andrews. He's from Newcastle. He actually seems really nice and wants us to go out for food. We'll see though..." I shrugged it off, not holding my breath and went to have a shower. By the time I'd come out I was met with a very excited mum.

"Oh my God Sophie! He's just signed to Manchester City!" she shrieked.

"What? Who?" My brain was still coming back to life
after a long lie-in and mum was looking way too giddy sat at
the computer. I staggered over to be greeted by a picture of
Josh's face filling the screen, as she began to read out the
latest online newspaper article. My first thought was "Great.
Not another one!" followed by excitement that this young
hopeful tipped for big things was interested in me. Optimistic
that he seemed different from the rest of them, then annoyed
that Mum had immediately Googled a guy I'd not even been
texting for 24 hours while I was in the shower. Did she do
that with every guy I spoke to? The way things were going, I
probably should do the same.

As one door closes, another one opens, and with Kane finally
recovered from his karma injury, he was promptly shipped
off on loan to some crappy lower league club miles away, so I
didn't have to see him or serve him again. This made space
in my head, heart, inbox and the restaurant booking system
for a new kid on the block: Josh.
He didn't come in to eat much during the week, but he soon
became friends with the young little rich boys of Alderley
Edge. They could compare Dolce and Gabbana trainers,
custom vehicle wraps and most of all, girls. Within days,
Josh was all over the news as the latest last-minute signing
for the England squad. He was set to hit the big time and I
prayed his ego, alongside all the desperate WAG wannabes,
didn't destroy him.
        Later that week we had our first date! I worked most
evenings so he took me for lunch at none other than Elixir.
The fancy club doubled as an even fancier restaurant in the
day through to evening and I'd always dreamt of eating there!
Anyone who's anyone would go there to be seen and pay an
extortionate amount for a mushroom risotto.

Although I was yet to meet the infamous former gangster owner, word on the hospitality industry street was he knew everything that was going on, even when he wasn't there. He knew exactly who was in his venue at any one time. Who they were, who they were with, what they were drinking, what table they were on, what team they played for and (most importantly) how much they were spending.

I got on so well with Josh and really felt like I was living the dream. I was beyond flattered that he was choosing to spend time with me, while paying for me to enjoy such an expensive rice dish. He was incredibly modest and I was honest with him that I understood very little about football. He even jokingly tried to explain the offside rule to me. We hugged goodbye and he asked did I want to come back to his for a cup of tea, then immediately apologised when he remembered he was out of milk. Could he be any sweeter? I giggled then politely declined, promising I'd join him next time when he had milk. I was also hoping this might secure a second date. It's ironic as nowadays I don't drink milk but hey, people change. Unfortunately for me, Josh was one of those people. And I don't mean a dairy dodger.

The weeks that followed consisted of him blowing hot and cold and standing me up. One of the most disappointing things in life (other than an over- cooked poached egg) has to be sitting on your bed alone, full make-up, fresh blow dry from the salon, a super cute new outfit that's been meticulously planned, all your giddiness and inner butterflies fluttering for your date night, only to be instantly replaced with the sinking feeling of rejection. It was a rare night off for me and to make matters worse, he texted me a couple of hours later to tell me he was having dinner with my friend, 'Sharkey' and they were talking about me.

'Sharkey' – real name 'Rob' – was one of the young rich kids in the village and had just inherited a football team. He was a regular at Fino on the days his live-in chef was off, and I'm sure he had lots in common with Josh. The fact that Josh would choose to hang out with him over me, then be dumb enough to tell me about it, made my blood boil with irritation.

I probably shouldn't have given him a second chance, but I did. Maybe he needed some 'boys time' and it was his lack of maturity or relationship experience that caused his bad judgement? Not realizing the disappointment he'd caused me, I would have a gentle word with him about reliability and communication at a later date.

That weekend he invited me round to his for that cup of tea after work. I wasn't too wary about going round. I trusted him and knew I could leave at any time, and I wouldn't stay late. I was also mega curious to see where he lived! Little did I know I'd practically been there before. Rich boy Rob lived in the same complex and I'd been to one of his famous house parties in his top-floor penthouse. I spent most of my time sat on the floor as I'd never felt under floor heating before, combined with such a thick, plush carpet. That was an experience in itself. Especially as I'd grown up with lino in the kitchen. I'd also delivered pizzas to other footballers in the same building, so when Josh texted me his address, I knew exactly where I was going.

He buzzed me in through the giant electric gates, then appeared outside in the shadows to walk me in. I should have been pissed off with him for standing me up during the week or at least make the point, but his shyness, cute smile and accent were enough to quickly make me forget.

His apartment was enormous! Complete with 12-seater dining table, pool table, framed football shirts on the wall, trophies, cinema-sized TV, wraparound balcony and the same under floor heating as in Rob's. I was very happy I opted to come here instead of the usual after work trip to Elixir. As much as I enjoyed chatting to the bouncers and all the customers I'd just seen in work, this scenario was definitely making my heart flutter more! We were both noticeably nervous so we talked for nearly two hours, sipping tea. I'm the sort of girl that will never make the first move with anyone. Even if I really like them, I won't do anything! I'll just wait patiently, hoping they like me too and will do something about it. After what probably felt like an eternity, he kissed me and those heart flutters rapidly went up a notch. Before I knew it, it was gone 2am and he was asking me to stay over. This was an absolute no-no for me on my first time visiting. For many reasons. Not just because I wasn't ready for him to see me drooling like a goldfish, washed up on land first thing in the morning. But judging by the way the past few hours had gone, I was certain that would be happening in the not-too-distant future. For that, I could hardly contain my excitement.

"No one has a bad word to say about you, it's so refreshing," he cooed, as he kissed me goodbye. "I can see why. We should do this again soon!"

"Definitely!" I smiled, as my cheeks burned with the usual wave of shyness that washes over me whenever a guy compliments me.

When I tiptoed out into my car, the dashboard clock lit up 2:45am It was like I'd been in a smooching parallel universe vortex the past few hours. I drove home in the biggest daze with a huge grin on my face. Things were working out perfectly and with my 21st birthday less than a month away, I had a feeling who I'd be spending it with. It was sure to be my most amazing birthday yet!

The odds of life continued to be in my favour and I was even getting more hours at work. They decided to train me as a cocktail waitress due to the constant busy bar area and people unable to get a table in the main restaurant. This was great as I didn't have the stress of seating bookings in an overbooked restaurant, when there were 320 booked and the only hope I'd have of fitting everyone in on time would be if they all inhaled their dinners in a matter of minutes. Or I maybe sat some in the disabled loo as overflow. By this time my tray skills were almost as good as my walking in insane heels skills and, as with any other type of waitressing, comes tips! I felt the jealous backlash of the other waiters on the floor though, as I had a smaller area to look after but was raking in more money. Particularly the night a Manchester United player and all his friends sat in the bar all night and gave me an £80 tip, despite me dropping a tray of Red Bulls on his head when a harassing wannabe WAG wouldn't move out of my way. That was the first time I'd seen a big pink £50 note. It was also the first time I'd seen someone with notes rolled up so tightly they resembled straws... but I chose not to question it and shoved them in my bra nonetheless. I didn't want any other staff to find out, resulting in more bitchy comments directed towards me.

"Come on then, how much did they tip you?" asked the trainee manager on duty, Susie.

"Ermm, I'd rather not say. I just tried my best and it's not a competition anyway..."

"Sophie, I'm the manager! I'm asking you!"

Jeez, this time last week she was just a waitress herself but now all of a sudden, she's wanting to know the contents of my bra.

"£80."

"Christ, did you give him a blowjob?!" she sneered.

"No! Like I said, I tried my best to offer them good service and as many beers as they wanted."

I was irritated by her comment and even more irritated when the entire team of servers knew within half an hour, and were all making similar sly comments. I tried to rise above it and danced it out at Elixir when I'd finished my shift. Despite the Red Bull spillage, I felt I'd nailed my cocktail waitress role and was looking forward to the thought of more tips!

I walked back to my car alone in the early hours, as I did most nights, knowing that crime was very low in this village, and I pretty much knew everyone and they knew me. I could outrun any drunk and if I got mugged, all I'd have to do was scream and someone would come running to my rescue, and they'd probably be a footballer.

When I arrived back at my car, I felt like screaming for another reason: Someone had ripped my windscreen wipers completely off! What kind of horrible person would do this? It felt like a hate crime and a personal dig at me. But who could it be? I didn't have any enemies and would bend over backwards to keep the peace with anyone. Everyone knew my car as — let's be honest — a pinked-up fluffy Ford KA stuck out like a sore thumb amongst the common Range Rovers or Ferraris of Alderley Edge. It really shook me that someone could be so nasty, and I massively take things like this to heart. The next morning I took it to the garage to be fixed and the bill came to (you guessed it) £80. Bye-bye tip!

For whatever reason, someone in that village didn't like me and I wanted to find out who, and more importantly, why?

Apart from the phantom wiper-swiper, other people in the village were looking out for me. However, they were saying things I didn't want to hear. Mainly, they were warning me

against Josh. In my eyes, we'd had a couple of dates, were
still texting amidst his busy training schedule and things
were progressing quite nicely. It wasn't until I caught him
out lying that I was forced to acknowledge his partying ways.
These people had clearly seen things I hadn't. As I did with
everyone, I wanted to believe he was good. He'd tell me he
was having quiet nights in, when in reality he was out
partying at seedy private parties or glitzy clubs. Assuring me
he couldn't wait to see me again and would rather catch up
on sleep to dream about me, while the rest of his teammates
were falling out of nightclubs. He was constantly inviting me
round late and last minute, which I know now screams
'BOOTY CALL'. But at the time in my deluded brain, I
believed he was just bad at planning. I could never make
these last-minute meet ups as I was working or would simply
rather have something planned in the diary with him so I
could at least be prepared.

"Sorry babe, I fell asleep early last night," he'd text,
after ignoring my messages.

Rich boy Rob was fast becoming 'Annoying nosey
Rob', as since he saw my car round at Josh's late that night,
he was always making crude comments or pumping me for
information.

"So have you slept with him yet?" Or "You do like
him, don't you? 'Cos he really likes you…" Classic wingman
style. I'd try my best to deflect and ask other things, like
what went down at the secret footballer party in a private
Manchester club the other night, of which the rumours were
rife!

"I wasn't there but Josh was, and he said it was
WILD! Loads of girls!"

My heart sank. Mainly because that was one of the
nights he'd put off seeing me and said he fell asleep early.
Why lie? I wasn't stupid. As much as he tried to convince me

that that wasn't his scene, it clearly was, so why not just own it? Instead of constantly telling me how he's 'just like me' and would opt for dinner and a movie over a club any day.

This started happening repeatedly. He'd make plans to see me, then cancel, claiming he wasn't well or had to be up early and I'd believe it. Until I'd see his car parked up outside the busiest bars or clubs as I drove home. I needed to bin him off completely out of my head, heart and hopes. Him going away for training in Austria with the England squad was the perfect chance for me to do this. Everyone warned me against him; I should've known he was just like the rest of them. I set my sights on planning my 21st, having only my true friends there and seeing it as a Josh-free fresh start. Obviously, it was going to be at Elixir, my home from home, and I'd dance and drink pineapple juice all night. Perfect! But I couldn't help but feel I had unfinished business and should give my Geordie footballer crush one last chance... As if he somehow had my brain tapped or could hear my thoughts, he started texting me again. All the way from Austria. Telling me about the altitude training with the England squad and, most of all, how much he was missing me.

"Your birthday's on the 30th isn't it?" He asked. I didn't think he'd remember.

"...And knowing you, it'll be at Elixir!"

I wasn't going to tell him, but he'd already sussed it and I immediately caved, the mere fact he even remembered my birthday.

"Yeah, that's the plan," I typed back. "And you'll miss it!"

"There's no way I'm missing your birthday, beautiful! I'm flying home on the 29th so I'll be there."

I nearly dropped my phone on my face as I lay on the sofa.

It pinged again: "Can't wait to see you xx," he added.

In that moment all was forgiven and I squealed with delight. Plan A was officially back on and spending my birthday with my reformed bad boy footballer crush was once again a reality! Apart from being unable to control the rest of the people that would turn up to the venue that night (annoying creepy guys or waiter Craig, for example), if most of the people around me were my good friends and my date, what could possibly go wrong?

Chapter 27 – Birthday from Hell

The best nights are the unplanned ones, so as much as I like
to be prepared (even if it's just changing my heels to even
higher ones, transitioning from hostess shift to dance floor),
I opted to keep my birthday plans quite simple: Open my
cards and gifts. Consume a lot of cake for breakfast. Spend
time with family and get ready for the main event at Elixir! I
texted round everyone I knew, knowing only 5% would
probably show. This was fine. As long as I had a dancing
buddy and Josh in close proximity, I didn't mind!

Elixir was packed and I got there early with my wingwoman,
Sophia. It wasn't long before Cheshire's elite and familiar
faces started pouring through the doors. These included a
couple I'd not seen in ages, colleagues who'd somehow got off
work early, most footballers who lived within walking
distance but still had a driver, and a bundle of loud giddiness
that was Air Hostess Chloe, and her part-time boyfriend Pilot
Dave. I was one sugar-free Red Bull in and having the time of
my life, yet not fully present. I was checking my BlackBerry
every five minutes and keeping one eye on the door for
Josh's appearance. Little did I know he'd already arrived,
halfway to wasted and was sat in a packed booth upstairs
with all his teammates and an obscene amount of vodka and
champagne. No text like, "Babe I'm here, where are you?"
Nothing. I waded through the sea of girls and drunken men
and tapped him on the shoulder to say hi. As he turned
around it's like he struggled to focus his eyes on me,
impaired by alcohol and distracted by the hundred other
girls.

"Happy birthday babe!" He slurred, giving me a quick
peck and promptly declaring, "I'm fucked already," as he
turned back around to carry on talking to his mates. This did

not bode well. I was determined not to let him put a downer on my birthday spirit so I proceeded to dance my socks off with Sophia on the neighbouring booth, where we could keep an eye on his drunken state. And, more importantly, watch him keeping an eye on me. It sounds pathetic, I know, but I bet you've done something similar yourself. Trying not to lose sight of that important person in a crowd while looking totally inconspicuous like you couldn't care less!
Sophia watched him watching me. Maybe he was sobering up and would decide to peel himself away from the lads and wannabe WAGs and actually hang out with me like he intended to. I'd pathetically ask Sophia if he was still looking, while I clung on to the last shred of hope in my heart.

"No, but wait. Don't look yet!" Sophia shouted down my ear, grabbing my arm. It was too late. I flung around to see what was distracting him and I wasn't prepared for what I was witnessing: he was sat down, being straddled by a girl as they shamelessly ate one another's faces. My heart stopped and then plummeted to my feet like a lift in a horror film when the cables snapped, right before everyone falls to their death and their insides fly everywhere.
"Don't look! Stop it! It'll make you feel worse!" cried Sophia. But in true horror movie style, I couldn't stop watching. When they eventually came up for air, my inner crashing elevator hit the ground hard when I realised the girl he was kissing was my so-called friend, Chloe. It was like I'd lost a friend, potential boyfriend and was granted the worst 21st birthday in history, all in a split second. I wasn't one for confrontation, so I immediately fled to the toilets to calm myself down and decided whether or not to call it a night and save myself more hurt, despite it only being 11:15pm.
"Having a good night?" asked the toilet attendant, who I'd often have the best sober chats with.

"Not the best," I sighed, at which point Chloe herself stormed in, in all her drunken glory, lipstick smeared across her face like the joker and a boob dangerously close to popping out to say hi. I didn't know where to begin with her. With the 'sisters before misters' mantra firmly instilled in me, I desperately wanted to salvage the friendship and believe she wasn't a bad person.

"Chloe, what are you doing? That's the guy I've been texting and had that lunch date with!" I confronted her calmly, trying not to cry. I hadn't told many people the guy I was texting and crushing on was Josh. I was a pretty private person and couldn't deal with the village gossip's fabricating their own version of the story.

"No way!" she slurred. "That's soooo funny, oh my God."

(I'm not really seeing the funny side here, love.)

"But Chloe, I'd really started to like him, and it's horrible seeing you kiss him! Can you just... stop!" My voice began to crack. Well done, Sophie, you sure told her. Not! Saying that to her was about as effective as saying it to a screaming toddler. She put her arm around me and lent all her drunken body weight into me.

"Don't be sad, babe. Let's have some fun and mess with his head a bit. He doesn't know we're friends," she winked, as she peeled herself off me. I figured because she couldn't see or walk straight, she probably wasn't thinking straight either. Whatever this 'game' this was, I didn't want to play it. I needed to get away from her and pull myself together. As I headed out the door, she shouted after me, "Remember! Let's play a game!" and she did that lazy drunken wink again as if her false eyelashes had stuck together.

The bar and dance floor had grown even busier in my short time in the ladies' loo, so I decided to throw myself into the sea of people, blocking any view of Josh and Chloe's behaviour, immersing myself in the music, even if I didn't like the song. Dancing out any negativity and rising above the bullshit. This was my 21st birthday for God's sake! One I knew I'd always remember, so I was determined to salvage it in some way. Sophia had to leave at midnight, but I was grateful she came out at all. By this point, I'd bumped into numerous other people I knew from the village, such as millionairess, Dina. She was the most chilled and down-to-earth person ever and immediately handed me a glass of Crystal for my birthday. With most alcoholic drinks, I'd normally chuck it in the nearest plant pot, but as my nerves and emotions were still all over the place while I tried to avoid Josh and Chloe, I decided to drink it. I hoped it would actually calm me down. But calming my nerves through alcohol made me feel like I was melting, like the witch at the end of the Wizard of Oz, having water thrown over her.

I NEVER drank, so when the offer came of a taxi back to Dina's for an after party with a load of others, I jumped at the chance. I was convinced I was drunk and wouldn't be able to drive, so I wanted to give myself a few more hours drinking water and cranberry juice to be on the safe side. I also didn't want to pass up the chance to party in a mansion on the outskirts of Alderley Edge, sandwiched between Britain's most loved cricket player's home and another premiership footballer's.

A group of us piled into a Mercedes minibus and twisted through millionaire's row after millionaire's row to our destination. It felt like the night was looking up after all.

Dina's house was literally a stately home! When I hopped out of the minibus I was immediately transfixed with the beautiful outdoor lighting, illuminating the huge windows, pillars, fountain and how ridiculously long her driveway was. Dina searched for her house keys in her personalised Chanel handbag, while we were rudely interrupted by drunken shouts and laughter, as another minibus full of after-party goers pulled up. Did they not realise they could disturb the crème de la crème of England's cricket and football teams who were sleeping either side? Clearly, they did not care. Dina rolled her eyes as she was largely sober and had the patience of a saint. I watched them all tumble out of the car, Birkin bags and Louboutins flying everywhere as the electric door was about to slide shut. That was, until a final couple emerged... It was Josh and Chloe.

Is this the universe literally trying to torture me?

I swallowed the lump in my throat and inhaled deeply as I turned away from their appalling display of zero morals, and stepped into the palatial marbled hallway. Surely this house was big enough for me to hang out in an entirely different wing to them, and I probably wouldn't even know they were there.

Like all good house parties, the kitchen was where it was at. We all kicked off our shoes, raided the fridge and got up on the giant marble island workshop to dance. A mega sound system blasted out Beyoncé in all the rooms as another glass of champagne was passed up to me from below, by an old guy I recognised from Elixir. Some of the others disappeared off to various living rooms to relax on the giant sofas or probably do cocaine in one of the nine bathrooms. I was happy dancing in the kitchen and all I cared about was that Josh and Chloe were well out of my eyeline. Painfully expensive glasses were getting carelessly knocked over by clumsy drunk people and Dina was incredibly blasé about it. I guess she could just buy more? She didn't even seem to mind that one girl had decided to start drunken cooking, and was making some kind of melted cheese monstrosity on the hob.

"Hey girls, if you want to get comfy there's a load of new Juicy Couture tracksuits in the first bedroom at the top of the stairs. Go and pick one," Dina offered. Something I would gladly take her up on as my tightly fitted outfit was starting to irritate me. It would also give me an excuse to check out some more of her house!

I crept up the sweeping staircase and was met with several beautiful oak doors, all closed. I tried the first one and it was yet another bathroom, because one can never have too many, apparently. I went for the second door, opening it into pitch black as I stroked the wall looking for a light switch. Bingo. The room exploded into a bright light and my inner elevator crashed once again... I'd walked in on none other than Chloe and Josh having sex. I froze as their heads popped up from beneath the crumpled duvet, only to immediately be tugged back over their heads like they didn't even care. I couldn't work out what was worse: the fact I'd just walked in on my so-called friend definitely NOT putting 'sisters before misters', my supposed date having sex with said friend at my 21st birthday afterparty or the fact he'd kept his socks on. It was all wrong on so many levels. I reversed out of the room, flicking the light off and stifling a vomit burp in my throat.

"What's up, chick, could you not find them?" Dina asked as I passed her in the entrance hall.

"No, there's...people in there," was all I could manage in response. I returned to the kitchen and sipped my second glass of champagne to calm my nerves once again which stupidly, in hindsight, only delayed me leaving even more, as my car was still parked miles away in the village. I certainly wasn't in the frame of mind to drive anywhere. Could this be the worst 21st ever in the history of 21st's?

I went and sat with the lads in the living room, half of whom were asleep. Once a very dishevelled looking Chloe was firmly back in the kitchen, the coast was clear for me to grab a tracksuit, so I too could have a nap and dream that all this hell would be over. I tiptoed back up to that sordid room holding my breath, not wanting to inhale their disgusting second-hand sex air. Sure enough, Dina did indeed have a spare bedroom wardrobe full of brand-new Juicy Couture tracksuits, all complete with tags. I grabbed the cutest one I could find. I was still technically 'Birthday girl' after all, so should still cling onto that sparkly image in some way. I took it to one of the many bathrooms to change, where I bumped into a topless Harriet, older sister of Rich Boy Rob, and clearly off her face.

"Harriet, are you okay? Where is your bra? And top?" I asked, genuinely concerned at how dazed and confused she was.

"Where's Josshhhh?" she slurred. I felt like abandoning the conversation right there but right on cue, he appeared in the hallway.

"There you are!" she shouted, grabbing him and pushing him into that same bedroom, locking the door behind them. I was almost not surprised and fast becoming immune to the grotesqueness of it all.

Desperate to escape but still convinced I was drunk and unable to leave, I took myself into one of the many of the bedrooms complete with blackout blinds, and decided to nap myself to a more godly hour of 7:00am, instead of the current 5:00am, where I'd then call a taxi back to my car before most of them woke up. I hoped. Maybe it was the glass and a half of champagne or sheer desperation to escape this horrible reality, but I did actually sleep. Only to be woken by an alarm beeping at 8:00am. I felt immediately terrible as I realised I'd taken Dina's room and hadn't even asked, but at least she still had seven others to choose from. Well, six, if you discount the sex bedroom of betrayal currently in use.

I crept downstairs and there were bodies everywhere. Smashed champagne flutes in the sink and solidified cheese on the kitchen floor. There were slightly fewer people than I remembered but it turned out some were in the garden, passed out on the patio furniture. Or comatosed on the floor behind the giant living room sofa. I thought I was the only one in the land of the living until I heard a water tap in the kitchen blasting on. I found Dina at the sink attempting to wash away small shards of broken glass. I normally would've offered to help or at least told her that's a really bad idea, but I needed to get out of there ASAP.

"Morning, hon," I whispered, not wanting to startle her. "Thanks so much for having me round, your house is beautiful! I'm gonna call a cab now if that's okay?"

"You're welcome, anytime babe! And don't worry, I've already called one. It should be here in 10, if you want to start waking people up?"

I really did like her and her incredibly laidback, accommodating nature, in spite of the fact her house was trashed and she'd never met half the people here. I gladly went to gather the others, knowing I sure as hell wouldn't be going to wake Josh up and whoever he was in bed with now. I never wanted to see him again and hadn't yet thought what I was going to do the next time he walked into Fino...other than smacking him in the face with the salt-crusted sea bass special.

"Taxi's here! Guys, come on! Quick. Let's go, let's go, let's go!" I shouted in a whisper as I dragged several people off the sofa and herded them out the door, like a mum on a school trip with a load of unenthusiastic, spaced-out teens.

As we shuffled out the door, squinting in the dawn light, I glanced over my shoulder and, to my horror, saw Josh staggering down the stairs like something from a zombie apocalypse. Please don't let him realise there's a taxi outside and please don't let him fit in it! I was begging praying in my head. We all squished inside in the most ungainly manner.

"Good morning! Is that everyone?" asked the annoyingly chipper driver.

"Yes! Yes, That's all of us. Drive please!" I snapped, having déjà vu of Sydney Harbour, when I escaped from that pervert on the ferry.

"Wait, there's one more coming out now...," some annoying guy in the back shouted.

It was Josh. Great. I watched in disgust, and my heart sank lower and lower, with every step he took nearer to the taxi.

It was the shortest but longest journey ever, and I'd never been more relieved than when that cab pulled up at the top of Alderley Edge High Street, and my trusty little car was there waiting for me. Josh paid for the taxi which, let's be honest, was the least he could do. I said goodbye to everyone apart from him and walked around to unlock my car door, desperate to drive off and scream very, very loudly.

"Bye, guys. Sick night, yeah!" he called to the others as he lingered by my car. I switched on the ignition. To my utter horror, my passenger door then flew open and he jumped in. Is the man completely retarded as well as shameless? I froze. I stared at him, waiting for him to get out again as this was clearly a sick joke.

"Give us a lift, babe. You're going past mine, anyway," he grunted. I wish I could say I slapped him, threw him out of my car while sounding my horn screaming "RAPE!" – or at least refused to drive anywhere until he got out. But I didn't. I was terrible at confrontation or being mad at people in general, and above all, I was more hurt than angry right now. Maybe this two-minute and three-second journey would give me chance to highlight how he'd made me feel, and what he and Chloe had done to me. I needed to find my voice and stick up for myself. I reluctantly pulled away from the curb, seething and dying inside simultaneously. The words didn't come and the world's most awkward silence ensued, only to be broken by him.

"Your mate Chloe's good fun. I didn't realise you two were friends..."

I glared back at him with an icy disgusted look on my face. Still the words did not come. I swung my car into his drive and yanked the handbrake on.

"There," I snapped bluntly.

"Wow, I feel battered," he slurred, slowly getting out. Pausing to look back in at me.

"I'm not surprised," I responded, wishing he would move faster as his presence was making me physically nauseous.

"Hey babe... Why don't you come in for a bit? We can pick up where we left off."

I kid you not! He went there.

"You're disgusting. Close the door!" I shouted. As that passenger door slammed, I threw it in reverse and berated myself for ever seeing anything in this scumbag of a guy. How could he even suggest that? It was grossing me out on every level.

When the sun broke through the hazy clouds on my first official morning of being a 21-year-old, I prayed the events of the last 12 hours would not set a president for my new year of age. But for as long as I was to stay working in this village, mixing with these people and being part of this scene, things weren't going to get any easier...

Chapter 28 – The Aftermath

Where do I even begin when people say, "How was your 21st?"

"Not bad" – "Great thanks!" or "Pretty uneventful" were my go-to's, then swiftly changing the subject. Unless it was a close friend, in which case they would get the full, gory details. Or if they were slightly irresponsible, they'd maybe try to persuade me to sell my story to a gutter newspaper. As tempting as it could be to make a quick buck, you only get one reputation, so don't ruin it by airing your dirty laundry in public. I had to think of my potential acting or presenting career, and I didn't want to be labelled or portrayed as a girl who (nearly) gets with footballers. Plus, imagine how mortifying must it be when your parents read those stories? Or their holy friends? I shudder at the thought of it.

The next few days could have been pretty bleak, but thankfully I was taken on a day out to popular theme park Alton Towers, with four of my fellow hospitality industry friends. It was the perfect thing to take my mind off Josh and my car crash birthday, repeatedly riding the biggest and scariest rides till you're almost throwing up your candy floss. I left my BlackBerry at home and unleashed my inner sugar OD'd child for the day. Everything was great until I got home and checked said BlackBerry, where, to my horror, I had a message from Josh.

"Hey babe, thanks for the lift the other morning. Can I have Chloe's number?"

Wow. Insert expletives here! Could he be any more of a scumbag? I was raging. There's so much I wanted to say, but it would be utterly pointless when dealing with such an imbecile. As this was in the days before screenshots, I immediately texted Sophia to tell her the latest level of 'low' he'd now stooped to. Once I'd calmed down, I eventually texted back a simple and blunt, "No. Get it yourself." Then I blocked his pin. I was dreading when he would next decide to turn up at Fino, unannounced, and force me to give him a booth because of who he was. Thankfully, he was out of the country most of the weeks that followed, so the only exposure I had to him was his ugly mug on TV. Or his huge face plastered all over the papers the next day for scoring goals for England. I'm not sure which was worst, to be honest. I felt like I couldn't escape him, and it only prolonged the feeling of anxiety for when he did eventually return and inevitably stroll into the restaurant. I didn't think I could handle it.

With the feeling of dread combined with an increasing number of bad shifts and Julie cutting the hostess hours, I made the decision to leave. It was a tough one. In typical Sophie style, I had nothing else to go on to and part of me still loved that little job. But there were far more bad times than good in the end. The good news was I'd amassed so many friends or 'acquaintances' in my time working there, and was so known in the village as 'Fino girl', I would still remain firmly part of the social scene, frequenting all the usual haunts. It was then that I got in with a group of local girls, who I naively believed were my friends. Oh, how wrong was I!

Before I was initiated into this glitterati girl gang of Cheshire, I was always surrounded by and hanging out with male friends. Flying solo most of the time and rocking up to venues alone, but knowing all the door staff and bartenders. I'd bump into multiple familiar faces once inside while dancing my socks off. It was on one of these particular nights that I caught the eye of a guy I'd not seen before. Throwing shapes in my usual haunt Elixir, I noticed I was being closely observed by a very casual man in a hoodie, hanging out in the DJ booth. (God knows how he got in here wearing a hoodie but hey, maybe he knows everyone in here like I do?!)

When he approached me and invaded my dance space, I was naturally irritated and on my guard.

"You're a great dancer," he grinned. "The best one in here."

"Thanks," I said bluntly, wishing he'd make his point and let me carry on.

"You're in here a lot, aren't you?" he winked.

"Most weekends. I'm surprised they let you in here wearing a hoodie!" Maybe over a year working on Fino's front desk had finally made me more assertive? Or maybe this was just me putting my foot in it yet again. He looked surprised, momentarily wounded, then shook it off and whispered in my ear

"Actually, it's OK because...this is my bar."

"Your bar?"

(Shades of the Andy Serkis chat in the green room were flooding my memory at this point.)

"Yes. I'm John. I own this place. And you are?"

I didn't know whether to run away to the toilets or apologise for my rudeness, but I managed to string some sort of sentence together like,

"Wow I'm sorry, I didn't realise! I'm Sophie. I love this place!"

"So I hear... Now, let me sort you out a drink while you tell me your number."

He was slightly creepy but dangerously charismatic, with hypnotic big brown eyes. I explained I didn't drink so the freshest cranberry juice appeared instantly, and I figured it wouldn't hurt giving my number to the owner of my favourite and most exclusive venue in the whole of Cheshire. I was aware I could be playing with fire here, though, as if the rumours were true, I was handing over my number to a former (and probably still current) notorious gangster.

He was friends with all the local footballers, celebs, drug dealers and millionaires, and promptly introduced me to anyone who was anyone in the bar that night. Another guy asked for my number too during that evening, and I felt like I was on a roll! I was rarely interested but I loved meeting people and networking, so who knew where it could lead?

Once I was home and all danced out, I received a text at 2:40am from a number I'd not yet stored.

"Sober Sophie... x" it read.

"Sorry who's this?"

"You don't even drink and you've forgotten me already?! Great."

Damn, this must be John. I felt immediately awful and frantically started backtracking.

"John! So sorry, hadn't stored your number yet! X"

"Well this is a good start!" he replied.

He was so blunt and sarcastic with a wicked sense of humour. I looked forward to seeing him in Elixir again and introducing my new girl clique to him. I'm sure he would approve! One was the daughter and heiress of a famous building construction company. Another was the daughter of the longest running and most successful Chinese restaurant in Manchester's Chinatown. One looked like a Rita Ora-Beyoncé hybrid, and the other didn't have to work and had a polo playing boyfriend called Hugo. Enough said. I couldn't help feeling like I'd pissed John off already, but hopefully I'd put all that right by turning up next weekend with all my fabulous friends.

Life wasn't just about going out, though. I was now jobless, living off sporadic babysitting jobs and was back to frantically applying for random castings on that lower league audition site. I went back to the presenting idea first and foremost, merged with a few commercial modelling castings, where I'd lie about my waist measurements as I had a naturally boyish figure. I was slim but straight up and down! I knew I was technically too short to be a model but if you had a pretty face and were all in proportion, I'm sure anyone would look great sat on the sofa in the DFS advert. Even if you weren't 5"11. Still, the presenting was my first choice. Being myself and not having to lie about anything... (hopefully!)

I saw a casting in Manchester for a Battle of the Band's style show, looking for a boy-girl presenting duo. Perfect! Edgy, quirky and I'd always had a huge love and understanding for music, coming from my ice dancing/ballet/ballroom/Latin dancing background. Not to mention watching countless hours of music videos on the music channels. Next stop, MTV Sophie!

Full of optimism, a self-styled outfit and a fake tan that wouldn't let me down this time, off I went on a tram into Manchester. Like always, I didn't know what to expect and I was slightly more apprehensive when I learned the meeting and casting location was down by the canal and the Piccadilly arches. It was a spot frequented by crack addicts, prostitutes or homeless. There weren't many other people there but the ones who were seemed so friendly and creative, if a little grungier than I was used to. I got partnered with a cool guy called Sam and after a quick hello, we took our marks in front of the camera. I carefully stepped over the discarded needles and prayed this wasn't the part where I got shoved in the canal, never to be seen again. Personally, I thought we were the perfect fit, but you always do when you're pumped full of confidence and adrenaline! Sam looked like a bass player from an indie band and we got on well from the get go. He was a breath of fresh air. A down to earth creative type, slightly shy and constantly ruffling his hair and dragging it forward across his forehead like the current 'Emo'/hipster trend required. It turned out he was a radio presenter for the cult online station 'Manchester Radio Online', and he was looking for a co-presenter.

"Come in and have a go if you want," he said, uber casually. "My show's 5 till 7pm on Saturday."

"Wow, yeah, I'd love to! I'll be there," I agreed, before I even knew where I was going or what I was getting myself into. But my initial gut feeling was 'Hell yeah, how cool?!' So I went with it.

When Saturday rolled round, I was kind of surprised to find the 'studios' were a tiny, smelly room above a grotty old pub in the rougher end of Manchester. Not the plush studios with sound proofing and pretty lights I was expecting. Instead, there was old carpet on the walls and three old microphones with decaying sponge muffs or spit shields. The pub landlord owned and ran the station and was passionate about putting on live and unsigned bands. Along with accommodating the local gypsy kings, alcoholics and general salt-of-the-earth, roll-up smoking northerners. It was worlds apart from the glitz and glamour of the Golden Triangle I was used to, but it did me good to mix with a different, more earthy crowd. Proper northerners, proper Mancs! I was aware that I could become sucked into the Cheshire scene and it would start to change me if I wasn't careful. Little did I know, I was already in over my head.

Despite no longer working at Fino, I found myself hanging out in Alderley Edge five nights a week or more. I'd never been 'in' with a group of girls before and when they said "jump," I jumped. We were all in a group BlackBerry chat, usually pinging utter crap or weekend plans. It would be a random Tuesday night and I'd be sat at home in a tracksuit, when suddenly the group chat would light up with a message from ringleader Sasha:

"Ladies! Hot chocolates at Blush bar at 7:30?"

Of course everyone was free to join, only lived a stone's throw away and had limitless disposable income for overpriced drinks and village parking. For me, this meant dipping further into my overdraft, taking a detour to pick up Zena as she was the only one who didn't drive, and frantically trying to pull together an outfit that screamed "WAG on a day off" or casual chic. It was always stressful, looking back. I had nothing in common with these girls and zero income to keep up with the constant meals out and meet ups. To earn my stripes and at least build some kind of deeper friendship with one of them, I gladly became Zena's personal chauffeur. This meant we'd have chats just the two of us and always arrived at venues and events together. We became really close, confiding in one another about boys, the other girls and our scarily similar experience with the local footballers. She didn't have a job either but was somehow decked out in the latest designer gear. It turned out she too had flirtations with footballer Kane and gangster bar owner John. At the end of any night out we'd often sit in my car, chatting for over an hour about everything that had happened. We knew all the same people and our experiences had been chillingly similar.

This was the start of a bizarre love triangle between Zena, gangster John and Sasha. One that I found myself in the middle of as designated driver or complete gooseberry on their weird 3-way dates. Basically, I think John wanted a hareem of much younger girls around him, and the fact we all knew each other made it very easy for him to manipulate the situation, playing us all off against each other. He'd invite us out for dinner at Manchester's most exclusive venues, where he'd order for us and we'd be treated like royalty. He'd take us to the sky bar and everyone would watch in amazement as we skipped the enormous queue for the lift. Any velvet rope was immediately unhooked when with him, and we'd be escorted up to VIP instantly. Every waiter, manager or bouncer knew him, and he was the exception to any dress code, forever wearing a hoodie or white T shirt. Sasha and Zena were both under his spell, and he watched as each of them vied for his attention, while he'd pick his favourite on the day and flirt with one and not the other. I've still no idea why I was even there at most of these dinners, apart from driving everyone. We must've looked like the oddest bunch or, heaven forbid, his escorts for the night.

On our first meal out together – the most I'd conversed with him since my initial "I'm surprised they let you in here wearing that" comment – it was noticeable he was slightly bitter towards me. I figured this was because I had declined his offers or ignored his flirtatious messages. He proceeded to subtly put me down or make me feel uncomfortable at any opportunity, as he did that night, when we all took our seats round the plush dinner booth.

I was already on edge and could sense an atmosphere that was far from relaxing or welcoming. A feeling only to be magnified by the conversations that followed. Once settled in our places around the table as directed by him, he looked over at me and said, "You dated Josh Andrews, didn't you? Have you been out with any other footballers?"

He'd watch as my eyes widened in shock and my mind went into overdrive, realising the rumours were true. Even though he wasn't there that day when Josh took me to Elixir for lunch, he knew exactly what was happening in his venues, where people were seated and what they were ordering. My heart sank at the thought that I might be perceived as 'one of those girls', yet here I was with my two new friends, who had both dated footballers and now had their sights set on John and his Manchester mafia- style powers.

The company you keep says a lot about you as a person, but I was just here for the free prawns! Which by the way, upon first bite, John proceeded to tell me I should never eat, as he insisted, "they eat all the shit at the bottom of the ocean," and would gradually kill me.

It didn't take me long to realise he was the ultimate control freak on every level, with chronic OCD. Telling the waiter exactly how he wanted his spinach steamed, sending back the garlic bread three times and complementing Zena on her outfit, but telling her how she could've made it slightly better. He'd order something, yet change it in every way possible. He changed his car every month, from Ferrari to Range Rover to Porsche, and he'd never miss a call on his stereotypical brick-like burner phone. Even during the dinners. He'd hold it close to his mouth like a walkie talkie, cupping his other hand over it so there wasn't even a chance of lip reading. I caught the drift of it sometimes and sure enough, he was being informed of the list of millionaires and celebs in his restaurant and what they were ordering...

"... And what's Dina drinking?" I heard him mumble.

Dina?! Dina was my friend, I was sure she wouldn't appreciate being spied on! John seemed to have eyes and ears everywhere.

After we had finished the meal, of course we were forbidden ordering dessert as "sugar with the devil." It was my job to drive us all to the cinema, where he had booked us VIP reclining leather seats with unlimited everything. He sat in the front of my pinked-up KA and preceded to change every setting possible, from the radio, to the air vents, to the head rests, all while slagging it off. He was almost as bad as my coked-up pop star passenger. Zena secretly went to see the film earlier on in the week so she could pretend she hadn't and impress John with her intelligence and accurate character predictions. While Sasha sat on his other side spitting feathers, trying to think of other ways to flirt with him. I'd spend most of the night rolling my eyes, but I was still willing to be there. Zena was my absolute BFF and a friend like I'd never had, so if by me playing chauffeur meant she could hang out with her crush more often, I was happy to help. Plus, enjoy these free VIP experiences! Having spent a year or more seating posh people in booths, it felt rather good to be sat in one myself.

Sasha and Zena became the ultimate frenemies, supporting and complementing each other to their faces, yet bitching about each other behind their back, while they both competed for the same guy.

My mum was highly suspicious of this John character and the potential that her daughter and friends might become embroiled in his gangster underworld. But I chose to gloss over the fact his famous restaurant and club got firebombed twice – two days after refurb, and that he was once in prison for manslaughter, almost killing a man. These days he drank beetroot and celery juice in the mornings and was often followed round by a small Chinese man, whom he told us all was his 'life guru and spiritual healer'. As nauseating as the three-way flirting was, my nights out with John and the girls were never going to be boring and that was something we could all agree on (to a point!).

Chapter 29 – Frenemies in Action

With most groups of girls comes most types of dramas. Especially when boys are involved, or sides are taken. Somehow by me being the most diplomatic, confrontation avoiding person in the world, I was the one they began to turn on. I started arriving late to the nights out so I could skip the expensive dinners and join them for a tap water and lemon later on. This meant I could do my online radio show with Sam, get changed in the pub toilets, then head across town to John's Manchester venue. It was like stepping out of one world then into another, from a world of stale, smelly, mothballed radio studio, interviewing passionate and talented unsigned bands, and broadcasting across Manchester's underground music scene, with the most genuine and unmaterialistic people; to a paparazzi-stalked venue full of any celeb that was in town and a magnet for the local wannabe WAGs or escorts. It was quite exhilarating! A constant shift in gears, and the feeling that I could throw myself in any social situation my life demanded and I'd probably be fine.

Manchester Radio Online was purely run and held together by volunteers, one of which I was proud to be. I treated it seriously as if it were a real job, hoping that one day soon I could actually earn money for talking on the mic. Sam was the one driving the desk though, so would often cut me off or cut me short. I figured this was a typical male and female presenter duo dynamic. Usually after the show, we'd go downstairs to the pub and Sam would start on the beer and I'd munch the free chilli nuts, while they'd ask me for more stories about the footballers who to them were household names, but to me were just pests with limited vocabularies. I quite liked my double life. One minute I'm the edgy radio presenter in biker boots and slouchy sweaters, the

next I was squeezed into a stretchy £10 LBD from H&M,
pretending it was Prada. My cheap throw-away fashion even
graced the dance floor of one of Mayfair's hottest clubs of the
moment, when the girls decided we should venture to London
for a weekend and remind ourselves there were other places
beyond Cheshire. I was excited yet anxious for that weekend
as Mayfair wasn't going to be cheap, and we were crashing at
an old friend of Sasha's. She hadn't seen him in years and
could since have gained a criminal record in that time or
developed a weird addiction. But.I'm sure he wasn't going to
complain at five gorgeous girls turning up at his house for
the night.

It was a strange setup as it turned out he didn't join
us on our evening out, but he did put us in touch with the
top club promoter who sorted us out a booth for cheap. Well,
cheap to the others. Not for me.

A night out in Mayfair was an experience and I
learned that a 'magnum' was not just an ice cream lolly. We
stayed at the club till the lights came on and went home via a
chicken shop in Kentish Town. Again, Sasha's friend was
loving life even more when five gorgeous girls returned back
to his, bearing chicken wings and nuggets at 4am. We
probably slept for all of two hours, then decided to get up
early and hit the famous Camden Market to drink in the sites
before driving home. Sasha was driving us in her brand-new
car, bought for her by her constantly harassing ex-boyfriend.
It should in theory have been a fun day out, but Sasha was in
the worst mood and calling all the shots, which was always a
bad combo. I'd not even finished my hipster vegan beetroot
burger when she demanded we set off home now, as she'd
had enough and was highly unimpressed with her falafel.
Tears followed as her ex- sent messages which obviously
triggered her emotions. I got the feeling I was not in the full

picture like the other girls, but I did my best to cheer her up while hoping not to unknowingly put my foot in it. More tears followed when we returned to her car to find she'd got a parking ticket, which she demanded we split between us. I didn't object to this. What I did object to was she took so long to pay it, it doubled in price, then demanded more money off us all. Later, I would put my foot down: it wasn't my fault she forgot to pay in time and I was seriously struggling for cash. (Unlike the rest of them.)

Looking back, several weeks on, this was the start of a big rift in the group. No one said "no" to Sasha, but here I was dropping that very bomb in the group chat. Awkward silences began and sides were taken. Zena sided with me (or so I thought), until it came to saving me from public humiliation. A humiliation she had the power to spare me from, but chose to watch me crash and burn...

It was Halloween Eve Eve and the nearest Saturday to the day itself. Naturally, this was the night everyone chose to celebrate and don their favourite costumes. Every year I was a black cat. Simple, sexy, something I could easily throw together. The year before I was at a house party in an Alderley Edge mansion and unbeknownst to me, ended up being a drug runner to my so-called guy mates. It went a little something like this:

"Soph? You're driving and sober aren't you? Would you mind driving us back to the village to pick up a friend?" asked Nathan's brother, who I didn't know as well as Nathan himself. But this was a small town and everyone knew everyone in some way. The party was pretty dull, so I didn't mind stepping out and playing taxi for half an hour. Pilot Dave came too and directed me to a backstreet house. I watched as Nathan's brother stepped inside and I recognised the man who opened the door: it was drug dealer Hush, still wearing his weird little hat even in his own house. I should have driven off there and then, but I foolishly believed the whole thing was innocent. I was confused when Nathan's brother jumped back in the car alone, telling me the 'friend' didn't want to come anymore. Maybe he felt uneasy getting in a car driven by a random girl dressed as a cat, with homemade ears on a headband and uneven whiskers drawn with cheap eyeliner on her face? Not to mention the sheer volume of pink accessories rammed in the car, Hello Kitty attached to the rear-view mirror and the pink feather boa draped across the back seat... I'd probably pass too if I was a bloke. After that pointless little interlude, I drove off back towards the party. Pilot Dave's phone rang and I immediately turned my music down so he could hold a conversation.

"Hiya mate! Yeah good, on my way back to a house party on the Edge. Why don't you join us? We've just picked up 10 grams..."

Ten grams. My heart sank. I might have been the one driving but I was the one who'd been taken for a ride. I was fuming when we arrived back at the party. I made it known I was pissed off. I was not my usual smiley, easy-going self, buzzing over fancy bottled water and had a face like thunder. Nathan, in his drunken stupidity, had the nerve to ask would I do it again for another two guys who didn't have the money for a taxi! Do I have 'MUG' written across my head? These people weren't my friends, and I sure as hell would never knowingly allow class A's in my car. I shortly left and got my car valeted the next day, to be sure there was no residue of anything. I vowed to myself next year Halloween would be better. And it was set to be! I had a group of girls to dress up with (albeit most of them now hugely frosty towards me since 'parking ticket gate'), and the chef's table booked at Elixir, thanks to gangster John who'd sorted the whole thing. He'd be dining with us before heading upstairs, where we'd all be hitting the dance floor, throwing shapes with a ghostbuster and suchlike. I'd recycled my outfit from last year but gave it an upgrade of thigh-high black boots, black tights and a leotard. I was now... Catwoman!

I had discussed my costume at length in the group chat and encouraged the others to get organised, as they casually said they'd decide on the night but would probably follow my lead. Even if the others didn't bother, I knew I could count on Zena to join me in the festivities.

We all know Halloween is also known as "Dress like a Slut" night for many girls. Or "cover yourself in dripping fake blood and you're good to go" night. For me, it was about striking a balance between fun, sexy, cute and UN-gruesome. I always avoided the horrendous sticky fake blood and those contact lenses that would float around my eyeball, momentarily blinding me. It was the one day of the year I could get away with having a tail pinned to me and wearing pretty much anything and it be deemed acceptable.

I was so excited to see what the other girls were wearing and I drove to Elixir like I stole my car. I was late setting off as I'd spent too long trying to take pictures of myself in the living room on a timer.

"On my way girls! Catwoman will be there shortly!" I BBM'd to the group.

I didn't get a reply but I knew it was because they were probably already there, marvelling at everyone's costumes, or more likely, the way John breathes.

I wonder what he'll come as? I would find out in due time.

When I pulled onto the cobbled path leading past the front entrance, I waved enthusiastically at the bouncers like I always did, as I followed the path round to the tiny and dimly lit car park at the back. I watched as other people made their way inside, not in fancy dress, and felt sorry for them and their boring life choices. I noticed the man in the driver's seat of the car parked opposite me, as he did a line of coke off the back of a CD case, his eyes rolling right to the back of his head. It made me shudder. I waited in my car briefly to be sure he was still alive. It was repulsive and terrifying at the same time, but I shook it off knowing I'd be hanging with the 'cool cat crowd' not the 'coke crowd'. One final check of my whiskers in the rear-view mirror and I was good to go! I tottered tentatively over the uneven ground in my black thigh-high heeled boots, then stopped as I felt my BlackBerry buzzing in my clutch. It was Zena messaging me privately, outside of the group...

"Soph, I don't know how to tell you this, but none of us are in fancy dress..."

"You're kidding?! I thought we all agreed we'd be dressing up! What happened?" I frantically typed.

Every second she didn't reply felt like an hour as I stood there dawdling in the shadows, looking like a lost alley cat. I guessed we'd discuss this when I got inside so I sent her another text to clarify.

"There are other people in costume even if you girls aren't though, right?"

"Babe, NO ONE in here is. I'm so sorry. I didn't know how to tell you and I figured it was too late when you said you were already on your way dressed as Catwoman," she replied.

"Zena, I'm stood outside dressed as a cat already getting weird looks, it's a bit late to tell me this now!"

"Shit! Erm... we're at the table now. What if you drove to mine and borrowed a pair of my skinny jeans to put over your leotard? Would that work?"

No, it would not. We both knew Zena was much skinnier than me and besides, how would I remove my

whiskers drawn on with industrial strength waterproof
eyeliner, and the tail I'd sewn to my leotard to prevent
annoying drunk people from pulling it off?

"Whereabouts is the table?" I asked. I wondered if I
could be discreet, dressed casually as a cat, and go mostly
unnoticed if the table was in the corner, tucked behind a
large pillar.

"It's the round one, right in the centre."

Great. The chef's table. The table where you could
see everyone and everyone could see you. I threw my phone
in to my clutch and took a deep breath. I had come this far,
spent ages getting ready and was fully owning and embracing
the fact that tonight I was a cat. More importantly I didn't
want to let them win or let them see their bitchiness had
ruined my night. I would rise above it, smile in the face of
embarrassment, float gracefully through the awkward
atmosphere around me. Yes, I would look like the butt of the
mother of all jokes, or Reese Witherspoon in Legally Blonde
when she turned up to that house party as a Playboy Bunny.
But tonight, I was a cat! And a sexy as hell one at that. I was
a cat that was going to show how confident I really am, and
how I cannot be broken by bullies!
I AM COMMITTED!!! With my inner voice screaming at me,
her preacher arms flying everywhere, I strutted in, keeping
my eyes fixed far into the distance. Imaginary blinkers on
and head held high. I was probably using up my lifetime
supply of balls in this very moment, unsure if they'd ever be
replenished. Or, if after tonight, would I be booking a one-way
flight out of the country? Deleting my Facebook and maybe
changing my identity?

"Wow, Sophie, you look... amazing!" laughed Sasha,
as she nearly choked on her vodka soda.

"Thanks!" I smiled, ignoring her insincere tone and
brushing my tail out the way as I took my seat. Zena leant

over and squeezed my hand under the table while looking me in the eyes mouthing, "I'm so sorry."

We'd talk later, I'm sure. Right now, I was still waiting for John's opening comment.

"You look like a twat." He smiled. "A lovely twat, but still a twat."

I felt my confidence draining out of my feet. Why was I doing this? I hid my face behind a menu as my cheeks burned redder than ever before. Conversation was a blur and I don't think I contributed much. I just drank my water and ate my side of tempura broccoli as it was all I could afford. Although John was paying, I didn't want to be indebted to him in any way. I observed the usual three-way flirting and competing between Sasha and Zena, along with John's severe OCD as he frantically beckoned over an available waiter.

"There's a pea on the floor under Table 5," he said. "Remove it."

Without saying a word and nodding confidently, the poor waiter hurried over and removed the offending pea, which the other diners were completely unaware of. It was the weirdest and longest dinner of my life and yes, I could have left at any time, but I was determined to make my point and salvage my night.

Thankfully, once upstairs on the dance floor, I became somewhat of a hit throughout the venue. The other dancers high fived me, cheering, "Go Catwoman!" Some even asked for a picture with me, much to the disgust of my bitchy girl clique. So much so, they all left early apart from Zena, knowing I was her lift home at the end of the night. Once I got over the nerves, the fear and the embarrassment, I literally didn't care anymore! It felt so liberating! I left all my inhibitions at the dining table and danced my tail off till the lights came on. Plan 'Humiliate Sophie and cause her to leave' backfired massively, and I was the star of the night. I was considering dressing like this every weekend.

By the time I drove Zena home, me being a cat wasn't even a thing anymore and I couldn't be mad at her. She clearly had my back after all, if she offered to get me emergency skinny jeans, and was happy to stay out with me.

I felt like I was nailing life, having learned the lesson of "Feel the fear but do it anyway," seeing how good things do come from taking risks.

Having said that, one life lesson I was still yet to grasp was sussing out who your true friends really are...

During this time of strained relationships, the one most pressing on my mind was that between myself and my bank balance. Yes, I was extremely busy and never in, but disastrous social gatherings and ordering overpriced side dishes as mains had seriously drained my bank account. I was filling my time going to the gym, ballet classes, weekend radio shows, baking, helping out at the dance school with baby ballet for extra cash, or sleeping in late to waste half the day. Being out of work can be really depressing as that feeling of having no purpose in life festers inside you. My little online radio show provided me with the perfect escape from loserville, as for those two hours, I was a radio presenter! I never had a problem with talking so that ticked the main box. It was refreshing to work with my grungy, plaid-shirt-wearing co-host and his grungy friends, who'd often jump on the mic as surprise random guests, and they'd usually swear as we weren't under Ofcom rules. Best of all, I could be completely myself. If this paid me, it would be my perfect job! But how you got to that point, I had no idea.

So, cue: mundane boring job just to earn some cash. It could've been worse. Far worse. But I wasn't prepared for the boredom, sore feet and pressured sales targets it brought. This came about thanks to a dear friend from the fragrance department during my Rackhams days. She put me in touch with an agency who supplies temporary staff to the make-up counters and fragrance halls. Back to my spraying people roots, and anything was better than being stuck in an office as far as I was concerned. Spreadsheets immediately caused my brain to shut down and still do.

Within days of my initial interview, I was booked on my first job in the centre of Manchester, at its largest low-end department store: Debenhams. I was thrust into working on a brightly coloured, very glittery make up brand counter, where I threw on a purple, branded T-shirt which read, "Ask me about how YOU can get bolder with colour!" and was sent out traffic stopping on the shop floor. Who in their right mind wants to be interrupted by a random girl holding a glitter eyeshadow palette, coaxing them to come downstairs to sit on the counter, and have green luminous glitter spread across their eyelids on a Monday morning? When all they're really here to do, is buy a 44F bra that doesn't chafe.

"You need to bring people back to the counter for me to do mini makeovers on!" whined the counter manager. "Wander round the store, grab them from other departments! Take the new lip glosses with you to entice them."

Who am I? The L'Oreal pied piper?

"And you're not wearing enough makeup!" she added, as she quickly pressed her shadow brush into my eyelids, covering them in black glitter.

With an unrealistic sales target of £380, I was going to have to sell a LOT of sparkly lip gloss and I wasn't even earning commission. I trotted round in my heels, approaching people with little success other than the homeless lady who was grateful for a bit of a makeover. I didn't care she wouldn't be buying. Eye shadow was probably the best thing that'd happened to her in a while. Unfortunately, she set off all the alarms and was wrestled to the ground by security guards, as she tried to shoplift half the counter and some branded men's boxers on her way out. Those automatic door alarms were always sounding, and it became apparent Debenhams had a huge shoplifting problem amongst its customers and staff.

"I ain't seen Shelly in a while..." someone would say, while eating with their mouth open in the staff room.
"She got caught shoplifting again. That'll probably be the last we see of her."

HOW had I gone from mixing with premiership footballers in one of Cheshire's most glamorous venues, to working at Manchester city centre's most down-at-heel department store? I later learned it went by the name "Dirty Debs" amongst other agency staff, who mostly only accepted shifts at the more prestigious stores like Harvey Nichols or Selfridges.
I hated every minute of Dirty Debs, and after receiving my first month of shifts, I requested I got inducted at the better stores so I could work there in future.
My nights out in Alderley Edge became a portal back to my former life and I lived for them. (When the girls didn't let me down or bin me off.) I found out on Facebook they'd all gone to Morocco and not invited me. I probably wouldn't have gone anyway after the Halloween episode, but Zena and I were still super close, so when I pinged her to express my feelings, she reassured me, saying it was super last minute, they were having an awful time and she missed me terribly. Thankfully, she wasn't gone for long as news dropped about an event that would grant me the sweetest revenge on scumbag footballer Josh and any other annoying player I'd

had the misfortune of serving. The tables were about to turn...

Chapter 30 - Payback Time

While the girls were away, floating round infinity pools and sipping out of coconuts, I was busying myself with ballet. I was taking part in a show at Stockport Plaza, as well as fundraising events with the radio and local charities. These usually involved unsigned indie bands and me running around with a bucket, its lid covered heavily with duct tape. It seemed slightly overkill, but it was in the rougher part of town where the bouncers wore stab-proof vests and someone would have absolutely stolen my bucket, if they knew how many fivers had been put in there from generous drunk people. I discovered how good I was at talking to strangers when it didn't involve me trying to put eyeshadow on them. Although I didn't realise it at the time, when I wasn't in the company of my toxic friends, it allowed me to relax and be more me. I had the chance to speak and be heard without trying to impress anyone, or fear of putting a foot wrong. I was carefree and real, and it showed me I was happiest and most relaxed in male company. Later in life, this transpired to me having more guy mates than girlfriends, which came with its own problems...but I digress. Back then, all I cared about was pleasing everyone, not having enemies or feeling like I'd upset anyone. Bending over backwards for other people and killing everyone with kindness, even if they treated me appallingly. If that sounds like you, let me warn you: it's the road to ruin.

My mum was really hoping after the Halloween episode, parking ticket gate and the fact they'd buggered off to Morocco without me, it would be enough for me to cast aside the 'friendship' and find some better friends. But no. When their plane touched down and queen bee Sasha pinged the group chat to arrange a 'welcome home reunion lunch at

Elixir' that weekend, I jumped. I figured it would give them chance to apologise, clear the air and explain their actions. It would also give me the chance to return to Elixir wearing something more than a leotard and thigh-high boots. Hopefully scrambling everyone's memory of my public humiliation. This time I would simply be the 'un-tanned friend' because I didn't go to Morocco. Rather than the 'didn't get the memo for no fancy dress' friend.

As well as mum berating me for my bad life choices, it was like the universe was too.

Prior to this Sunday afternoon reunion lunch, I decided to go to the gym and work up an appetite. I slipped and fell flat on my back while running in the entrance, which made for an embarrassing workout and some light entertainment for the people on the cross trainers.

"How misfortunate," I thought. My stubborn self, carrying on regardless. Then later on (and more bizarrely), as I turned in to the cobbled driveway leading up to Elixir, the world's biggest tomato was thrown out of nowhere at my car, splattering across my windscreen and temporarily blinding me. I screamed, fearing someone's spleen had just dropped out of the sky. I turned my wipers on then carried on to the back car park and my usual spot. I had no idea who had thrown it, where they came from or where they disappeared to. I never saw it coming, rather than thinking "Maybe God's trying to tell me something?" Like I shouldn't be meeting up with these girls, and was literally walking into the lion's lair! But I carried on regardless.

Surprisingly, they were sickeningly nice and no one mentioned my lack of ears and tail. Besides, we had more important things to talk about. Not Morocco or where was my invite, that was in the past and I was enjoying the less frosty reception. Not the phantom tomato thrower or my disastrous trip to the gym. Oh no, we were here to discuss the absolute talk of the town event...

John and Elixir were putting on a 'Celebrity Cook-off', featuring the top premiership football teams and their players. All to raise as much as possible for a local children's charity. The players would be battling it out in the kitchen, behind the bar and on the restaurant floor, as they served the wealthiest (or some could say "bravest") of diners. It was thousands to secure a table and they were nearly all taken, as many would give their right arm to be waited on and rub shoulders with their favourite players. Obviously, I couldn't stand footballers and was sick of the sight of them since my time at Fino, BUT! I saw this as an opportunity I would absolutely relish... An opportunity for them to serve me for a change! Oh, how sweet this would be! I couldn't afford a seat in the restaurant, but lucky for me, bar tickets were still available at an eye-watering but doable £50 a piece. Even luckier for me, who would be taking part and listed as one of the bar team? None other than Josh Anderson.

The other girls didn't seem fussed, but Zena and I were struggling to contain our excitement! She was on-and-off dating the Turkish equivalent of David Beckham and he too was taking part. (Sadly not actual David Beckham but hey, we can't have it all.)

Sasha didn't fancy it as her ex was bound to be there as a footballer's wingman, and the others were potentially going to St Barts or Turks and Caicos with family. Music to my ears. Just me and my wingwoman, Zena, then. I could picture us now: sitting at the bar as I gave Josh absolute hell. Being the world's most awkward customer, ordering off menu, elaborate non-alcoholic cocktails which required him to peel blueberries, then hating everything he made me and demanding he make me something else. Every sip would taste like sweet revenge, while I'd watch the beads of sweat develop on his brow as he grew increasingly more flustered when he couldn't find a fresh carton of cranberry! This was what I'd been waiting for and I never even knew it could happen in such an entertaining way.

In the weeks running up to the big night, the planning of military precision began: the outfit, the extensions, which way to curl my hair, when to start building up the tan to ensure optimum colour on the night itself. Phrases to use when sending back my cocktail as I'd never complained in a restaurant in my life. All the intricate details! But most of all, I had to look absolutely killer. Various potential scenarios of the night playing through my head got me through many a dreary shift at Dirty Debs, while I wandered aimlessly round the shop floor with my glorified clown make-up. I'd not seen Josh for ages, thankfully, only from a distance with slaggy drunk girls draped over him in faraway booths. And I certainly didn't ever have to fear running into him in Debenhams.

The lads at the radio couldn't believe the plans for this extravagant charity cook-off, but were content reading about it in the newspaper the day after and getting the real inside scoop from me the weekend following. They thought my double life was mental, yet they didn't even know the half.

The day finally came and I was pretty sure no one quite understood my excitement other than Zena, mainly because she's the only person that knew the full extent of the utter horror I went through with Josh.

The Premiership Cookoff was the hottest ticket in town and many people couldn't get in, but Zena and I waltzed in with a smug look on our faces, seating ourselves on the perfect bar stools, front and centre. We were very early but this was no ordinary night. I was also enjoying the fact my other frenemies were out of the country, directing their bitchy behaviour at someone other than me. A loud voice boomed out through the speakers, introducing the teams and players, and they all filed out into position, complete with white shirts, aprons and little notepads in their pockets for taking orders. They looked every inch the waiters. The only thing giving them away were the Rolexes, super rare Nikes or the occasional gold tooth. Josh looked less than thrilled to be there and I wasted no time in making his experience even more testing. Being vague about my order, sending it back twice and watching gleefully as his chaperone bartender barked orders at him to work faster, as a sea of people pressed their bodies up against the bar. Leaning over trying to give their order, they grew increasingly more impatient. I couldn't afford to order many £10 mocktails but I was even making tap water more hassle than needed, requesting it to be colder or with thinner slices of lemon. The whole experience only lasted about an hour, but I loved every second of it! Before I could finish my overdramatic tap water, the players had finished their serving duties and were dragged through to the dining area to take part in the charity auction, where Josh bid on a night out with a famous glamour model. I wouldn't have expected anything less.

Once upstairs on the dance floor, I noticed Elixir was filled with a whole different crowd, not the same old faces of the same people, week in week out. A different type of celebrity, out-of-towners and all the cool or edgy looking friends or family members of the players taking part. I soon got chatting to a flamboyant looking guy wearing a velvet blazer. He was from LA of all places, and had the dreamiest accent.

"How did you end up in Alderley Edge then?" I asked, knowing full well where I'd much rather be!

"I'm here supporting my buddy. He was waiting on tonight. He did awesome! Here, let me introduce you to my friends... Guys!" he shouted, beckoning over a group of the most handsome, tall and well-dressed men I'd ever seen. As they all introduced themselves, not one of them was British and I was not at all surprised. They oozed a different kind of charisma, style and (let's be honest) height, that I was yet to find in most British men. My velvet-clad friend introduced us all then quickly took off across the dance floor to chat and dance with other girls. I got talking to one of the tallest ones, who told me he was from Texas but had moved here while his brother played for one of the largest northern teams. I couldn't help but think they all must be horrified with the state and behaviour of British girls, their drinking habits and overall lack of ladylike class. The conversation was effortless; our eyes locked. I became oblivious to everything else going on around me. The rest of the group had dispersed, and it was just him and me.

"Wow. He's so handsome!" my inner voice screamed. My speech probably slowed, like everything else around me and I couldn't get over how Ken-doll like this guy was! Just a year older than me but with a confidence and aura beyond his years. Ethan – 22, from Texas – was a dreamboat. Our little chat, which had turned into quite a big one by this point, was interrupted when his brother appeared, having changed out of his waiter's attire. It was high fives and "awesome's" all round, and Ethan introduced me. His brother was equally friendly and polite, yet half the size, despite being the 'big bro'. I'd lost Zena at this point but I soon bumped into her in the loo and we had a debrief. After coming off the back of one catastrophic disaster with a guy, I didn't want to get my hopes up or get involved with another one so soon. Maybe I would become a nun like my mum always joked she wanted?!

Although it was hard, I decided to distance myself from Ethan a bit and concentrate on doing what I do best: dancing and being a carefree spirit with my bestie. When he came and found me though, to ask for my BB pin, I practically verbally gushed all over him.

"Come on dude, we're leaving!" shouted his older brother, who was annoyingly calling the shots.

"Ah shoot, look, I gotta go, but I'll ping you and we'll hang out," he said, while kissing me on the cheek, saying how nice it was to meet me. I melted. Then quickly pulled myself together, building my wall up again.

Zena got a lift home with her Turkish beau so I drove home alone, feeling highly satisfied with what I'd achieved that evening. Plus, the added bonus of meeting a real-life Captain America. I'd never felt such an instant connection with anyone before in my life. It's quite terrifying. I was managing my expectations, telling myself I'd probably never hear from him again. But I would make sure my BlackBerry never left my side for the days that followed, apart from when it was held hostage in my locker at Dirty Debs.

On the subject of hostages, I guess my heart still was one, trapped in a room of hurt and disbelief of what I'd experienced these past few months. Years even. Not just from Josh, but the beatings my heart had taken from all those people I'd once held so dear: friends who'd turned into foes, colleagues and coaches who I once believed had my back. I hoped I'd break free from this prison of negative thoughts and feelings that were holding me so tightly against my will. I could nearly see my way out though, and that way was Ethan. This was either going to be the biggest adventure of my life, or something that would slowly destroy me. There would be no in-between.

So, in the meantime, I'll just wait. Wait for that message to ping.

To be continued...

9 781739 379605